Getting into Secondary Teaching

You might also like the following books from Critical Publishing

Success! Passing the Professional Skills Tests for Teachers
Jenny Lawson, Annabel Charles and Trish Kreft
978-1-910391-01-3

Understanding and Supporting Behaviour through Emotional Intelligence
Victor Allen
978-1-909330-77-1

Our titles are also available in a range of electronic formats. To order please go to our website www.criticalpublishing.com or contact our distributor, NBN International, 10 Thornbury Road, Plymouth PL6 7PP, telephone 01752 202301 or email orders@nbninternational.com.

Acknowledgements

Figure 9.2, A four-dimensional framework of teacher resilience, is reproduced by kind permission of Elsevier Limited from Mansfield, C, Beltman, S, Price, A and McConney, A (2012) Don't Sweat the Small Stuff: Understanding Teacher Resilience at the Chalkface, in *Teaching and Teacher Education*, 28(3): 362.

Getting into Secondary Teaching

 Edited by Andy Davies & Mel Norman
Series Editor Andrew J Hobson

CRITICAL
LEARNING

First published in 2016 by Critical Publishing Ltd

British Library Cataloguing in Publication Data
A CIP record for this book is available from the British Library

ISBN: 978-1-910391-34-1

This book is also available in the following ebook formats:

MOBI ISBN: 978-1-910391-35-8
EPUB ISBN: 978-1-910391-36-5
Adobe ebook ISBN: 978-1-910391-37-2

Cover and text design by Greensplash Limited
Project Management by Out of House Publishing
Printed and bound in Great Britain by TJ International Ltd.

Critical Publishing
152 Chester Road
Northwich
CW8 4AL
www.criticalpublishing.com

MIX
Paper from
responsible sources
FSC® C013056

Contents

Meet the editors

Andy Davies is a principal lecturer who is programme leader for postgraduate secondary pathways at the University of Brighton. Andy taught history and politics in secondary schools in Oxfordshire and Surrey and has experience as both a pastoral and curriculum leader. Andy moved into Initial Teacher Education in 2009 and is currently researching government policy regarding the place of higher education in teacher education.

Mel Norman has taught in schools as head of geography, head of year and assistant head. Since joining the University of Brighton, Mel has been programme leader for both undergraduate and postgraduate courses and is currently the route leader for PGCE Geography. Her doctoral research focused on the construction of the school curriculum.

Andrew J Hobson is Professor of Teacher Learning and Development and Head of Education Research at the University of Brighton. He has previously been a teacher and mentor to newly qualified teachers. His research is concerned with the professional learning, development and wellbeing of trainee and more experienced teachers.

Meet the authors

All of the contributing authors work at the University of Brighton in the School of Education, apart from Nickey Brown and Mark Boylan who work at Sheffield Hallam University (SHU) in the Department of Teacher Education and Paul Dickinson who works at Leeds Trinity University in the Institute of Childhood and Education.

Mark Boylan is a reader in teacher education at Sheffield Hallam University. His background is in secondary mathematics teaching and mathematics initial teacher education. He undertakes evaluation of large-scale professional development projects and researches and writes about ethics and social justice in teacher education.

Nickey Brown is a senior lecturer in education at Sheffield Hallam University. She is course leader for the PGCE in modern languages as well as curriculum and assessment lead for modern languages, Teach First. She teaches on both courses and works with beginning teachers in schools as an academic tutor. She has previously been a teacher and mentor to trainees and newly qualified teachers. Her special interest is emotional engagement and she has developed materials to support the SEAL (Social and Emotional Aspects of Learning) programme as part of a DFID funded project.

Paul Dickinson is Director of the Institute of Childhood and Education at Leeds Trinity University. Previous experience includes head of teacher education at Sheffield Hallam University, teacher of English in four different 11–18 schools and external examiner for initial teacher education programmes. He was co-editor of Clarke, S, Dickinson, P and Westbrook, J (2010) *The Complete Guide to Becoming an English Teacher*, and in 2014 presented in Norway with J Silvennoinen (Helsinki University) comparing English and Finnish secondary teacher training.

Sally Johnson is a senior lecturer at the University of Brighton leading the PGCE secondary art and design course and is also the art subject co-ordinator. She has taught art and design in a range of secondary schools and FE settings. She has also worked as an art specialist in the primary sector and been involved in training teachers across both sectors. She continues to facilitate specialist workshops and write materials for the classroom.

Brian Marsh is a principal lecturer in education at the University of Brighton. Having had extensive experience in a wide range of schools he now leads the PGCE science team and also teaches on the MA and EdD programmes. His areas of active research include the professional development of trainee teachers in school-university partnerships as well as the professional learning of teachers particularly through the use of video technology.

Karen Murray-Hall is a senior lecturer in education at the University of Brighton, where she is academic lead for the PGCE (secondary) as well as route leader for modern foreign languages. She also lectures on a number of undergraduate modules in primary languages. Prior to this she worked in initial teacher education at the

Open University. She has also worked as a teacher of modern foreign languages and personal social and health education (PSHE) for many years in a variety of secondary school settings.

Tom Newlands taught in a number of secondary schools before working at the University of Brighton as a teacher educator on both primary and secondary courses. He leads the secondary PGCE religious studies (RS) route and is assistant programme leader for the secondary PGCE programme. His research in the past has focused on spiritual education in RS and he is currently researching teacher autonomy In the early career of secondary RS teachers.

Sarah Poore has many years of experience as a secondary science teacher and is now a senior lecturer in science education at the University of Brighton. She is passionate about creative and engaging science teaching. She works with secondary ITE trainees and undergraduate courses specialising in coaching trainees in school. Her research interest currently lies with helping school-based mentors and trainees to reach a common understanding of how to develop trainee teachers' skills.

Bhavna Prajapat worked as an interior architect, a teacher and a mentor for trainee teachers before working in initial teacher training for primary and secondary age phases. She teaches on both undergraduate and postgraduate courses at the University of Brighton as a design and technology specialist. She has been involved in supporting continuing professional development of teachers for many years as well as being a consultant for curriculum planning.

Steve Roberts is a senior lecturer in English. Before working in postgraduate initial teacher education, he was a subject leader In English, teaching in secondary schools in London and the south-east of England. He is interested in developing teachers' awareness of multimodal communication and drama as a learning medium.

Gary Stidder is the PGCE, School Direct and Troops to Teachers route leader for physical education at the University of Brighton. Gary is the co-founder of the University of Brighton's pioneering 'Football 4 Peace International' which has been operating since 2001 in Israel, Palestine, Jordan, Northern Ireland, South Korea and The Gambia. In 2013 Gary was awarded the University of Brighton's award for staff excellence in community engagement in recognition of his contribution to widening participation.

Chris Sweeney is a senior lecturer in secondary education, specialising in computing. He teaches both subject and professional studies modules on a range of courses from foundation level, as well as BA, PGCE and Masters degree courses. With over 25 years' experience in education, he has worked with a range of schools across the south of England, supporting trainees' professional development during their training. His research interests include professional identity development and social class.

Series editor's introduction

This book provides readers with an expert, comprehensive and up-to-date account of the process of getting into secondary teaching. It is an invaluable source of guidance for those who are considering embarking upon the process of becoming a teacher as well as those who have already begun such a voyage. I noted in my Introduction to this book's sister publication, *Getting into Primary Teaching*, that the decision to become a teacher must not be taken lightly, and I would perhaps lay even greater stress on this point in relation to secondary teaching.

The experience of becoming and being a teacher in secondary schools is an extremely challenging one, regularly involving both *'delightful highs and distressing lows'* (Bullough, 2009, p 34), associated with feelings of enjoyment, excitement, hope, satisfaction and reward on the one hand, and vulnerability, fear, frustration, humiliation and despair on the other. As my colleagues and I found in the 'Becoming a Teacher' research project in England (Hobson et al, 2009), and as I recall from my own experience as a beginner teacher, there are numerous causes of such feelings, which impact on secondary teachers' well-being, job satisfaction, motivation and willingness to remain in the profession. These typically include: witnessing one's positive influence on students' learning and development; positive or negative relationships with both students and teachers; student behaviour; workload and work–life balance; and the extent to which teachers feel competent, autonomous, trusted and supported by mentors and others, on the one hand, or are subject to relentless monitoring, evaluation or changes in government policy on the other.

All of these factors and challenges remain, and the editors and authors of the various chapters of this book have witnessed them at close quarters and have helped a very large number of student and more experienced teachers enjoy and come to terms with them, respectively. These writers boast decades of experience of working as secondary teachers and leaders, preparing (supporting, educating and training) new secondary teachers, and supporting the professional learning and development of more experienced teachers. They are highly committed, expert practitioners and teacher educators, subject specialists, and researchers.

As well as their own considerable knowledge and experience, the authors of the chapters also draw on the latest research and on the recent experiences and 'voices' of student teachers, experienced teachers and school leaders, to illustrate and help explain key aspects of learning to become – and being – a secondary school teacher. This, together with the use of real-life examples and the reflective tasks provided, makes *Getting into Secondary Teaching* a highly informative, engaging and enjoyable read.

In keeping with the underlying principles of its publisher, Critical Publishing, the authors of *Getting into Secondary Teaching* stress that those considering becoming teachers would benefit from developing – or developing further – an informed *critical, analytical and reflexive* approach to teaching, education and (for those who do make the decision to undertake a teacher training programme) their own professional learning, development and well-being. This is important because it enables you to develop *'learnacy'* (Claxton, 2004), that is, the ability to learn from your own and others' experiences and from other sources, which in turn will help you to become and remain a good or excellent teacher. It is important to recognise that this will not happen overnight. Teaching is much more than learning and 'delivering' a body of knowledge, and becoming an excellent teacher requires much more than learning from trial and error or from being apprenticed to an existing excellent teacher. Among other things, it also requires:

o *understanding* – for example, of how different students learn, of various barriers to learning which different students experience to different degrees, and of the means to potentially overcome such barriers;

o the discovery and development of your own personal *teacher identity*;

o the discovery and development of your own *unique* approach(es) to teaching and facilitating learning;

o continual *evaluation* and *adaptation* of such approaches for different learners in different contexts; and

o the development of *resilience* and mental strength, to enable you to cope well with the everyday demands and to 'bounce back' from the inevitable lows associated with becoming and being a teacher.

Getting into Secondary Teaching addresses all of these important matters, while providing invaluable insights into a range of other key concerns pertinent to becoming a secondary school teacher, including:

o what it is like to teach in different kinds of secondary school and what it means to be a professional;

o which type of initial teacher preparation programme (commonly referred to as 'Initial Teacher Training' – ITT, or 'Initial Teacher Education' – ITE) might appeal to different potential applicants;

o the changing policy landscape in education and its impact on secondary teaching and teachers;

o the nature and demands of professional learning as a teacher;

o the nature and importance of subject knowledge, and developing as a subject specialist teacher;

o developing classroom management skills;

o working with young people as part of the pastoral systems of schools;

o the importance of 'emotional intelligence' and other factors associated with thriving as a secondary teacher; and

o how to apply to and seek to secure a place on an initial teacher preparation programme.

I hope that you will learn much from reading the following chapters, and that they will be immensely helpful in enabling you to make an informed decision about whether secondary teaching is for you. For those readers who make the decision to embark upon this potentially treacherous yet exciting and rewarding voyage, *Getting into Secondary Teaching* will also help to prepare you for the enticing, exhilarating and stormy waters that lie before you.

Andrew J Hobson, 2016

▶▶ **FURTHER READING**

The following sources, based on the 'Becoming a Teacher' research and the experiences of just under 5000 student teachers in England, provide further insights into the nature and challenges of undertaking an ITT or ITE programme, and into ways of addressing and overcoming some of those challenges:

- ○ Hobson, A J, Malderez, A and Tracey, L (2009) *Navigating Initial Teacher Training: Becoming a Teacher*. London and New York: Routledge.

- ○ Malderez, A, Hobson, A J, Tracey, L and Kerr, K (2007) Becoming a Student Teacher: Core Features of the Experience. *European Journal of Teacher Education*, 30(3): 225–48.

In addition, the following title is an inspirational and aspirational read on the journey of becoming a teacher:

- ○ Boyd, P, Hymer, B and Lockney, K (2015) *Learning Teaching*. Northwich: Critical Publishing.

The sister book to this one is about getting into primary teaching and useful general material on applying for teaching programmes, including the Skills Tests, the nature of learning, and inclusive teaching:

- ○ Owen, D and Burnett, C (eds) (2014) *Getting into Primary Teaching*. Northwich: Critical Publishing.

REFERENCES

Bullough, R V, Jr (2009) Seeking Eudaimonia: The Emotions in Learning to Teach and to Mentor, in Schutz, P and Zembylas, M (eds) *Teacher Emotion Research: The Impact on Teachers' Lives*. New York: Springer, 33–53.

Claxton, G (2004) Learning Is Learnable (And We Ought To Teach It), in Cassell, J (ed) *Ten Years On: The National Commission for Education Report.* [online] Available at: http://challengepartners.org/challengethegap/uploads/media_one/afd78-Learning-Is-Learnable.pdf (accessed 28 May 2015).

Hobson, A J, Malderez, A, Tracey, L, Homer, M S, Ashby, P, Mitchell, N, McIntyre, J, Cooper, D, Roper, T, Chambers, G N and Tomlinson, P D (2009) *Becoming a Teacher: Teachers' Experiences of Initial Teacher Training, Induction and Early Professional Development.* Nottingham: Department for Children, Schools and Families.

Jargon buster

Ability grouping: pupils may be organised into groups according to individual ability assessed by various tests. Pupils may be grouped into 'sets' where it is possible to be in a higher or lower set according to their ability in each separate subject. When pupils are 'streamed' by ability there is less flexibility than with setting, with pupils placed in a higher or lower group for all subjects across the curriculum.

Academic curriculum: the range of subjects taught in school which can lead to external qualifications such as GCSEs and A levels.

Academic tutoring: part of the role of being a form tutor (see below) where the academic progress of individual pupils is regularly monitored and discussed.

Academies: publicly funded independent state schools with the freedom to set their own curriculum, school day, term dates and conditions of employment for staff.

Assessment: gathering and recording information regarding pupil progress and attainment. The process of defining the development of knowledge, skills and understanding.

Behaviour management: relates specifically to the strategies the teacher has in place to ensure pupils behave in a manner which enables everyone to engage in learning.

Classroom management: the wider context of managing the whole learning environment, with attention to risk assessment and the health and safety of the pupils. Thus, it includes consideration of the arrangement of the tables and chairs, pupil access to books and other resources, general classroom rules such as being out of one's seat, storage of pupils' bags and coats to prevent accidents, and safe arrangement of electrical equipment to avoid pupils tripping over electrical cables.

Coaching: in the school context, support provided for a teacher's professional learning and development, often focusing on specific skills and goals. The word is sometimes used interchangeably with 'mentoring' (see below).

CPD: Continuing Professional Development — the expectation that once qualified, teachers will continue to further their professional development by engaging with courses, conferences and other activities to keep abreast of developments in both the specialist subject and education in general.

CTCs:
City Technology Colleges

these were established in urban areas in the early 1990s to enable pupils to focus on technology-based subjects, including mathematics and science, working in close liaison with local businesses.

Curriculum:

the subjects taught in schools (academic curriculum) and aspects relating to non-academic subjects like PSHE (the pastoral curriculum; see Chapter 8).

Cyberbullying:

threatening people via use of texting, Facebook, Twitter or other computer-based technology.

DfE:
Department for Education

the government department responsible for education and children's services in England.

Differentiation:

tailoring planning and teaching to meet individual needs so all pupils in a group have the best possible chance of learning.

EAL:
English as an Additional Language

applies to pupils whose first language is other than English.

EBacc:
English Baccalaureate

a school performance measure indicating how many pupils achieve grade C or above in the core academic subjects (English, mathematics, history or geography, the sciences, a language) at Key Stage 4 in government-funded schools.

Emotional intelligence:

the capacity to be aware of, control and express one's emotions, and to handle interpersonal relationships judiciously and empathetically.

e-safety:

making people aware of the hidden dangers of the internet and social media.

Evidence-based teaching practices:

term used to describe the use of (e.g.) educational research and practitioner inquiry to influence teaching and learning.

Faith schools:

schools associated with a particular religion. They can be academies, maintained or free schools.

Form tutor:

having responsibility for a group of pupils beyond subject specialist teaching.

Free schools:

schools funded by the government but free to develop their own curriculum and priorities.

Grammar schools:

in local authorities where grammar schools still operate, pupils have to pass an exam to gain entry to a grammar school. This test is known as the 11+ and pupils who achieve a high enough pass mark in this test are awarded a place at a grammar school. Some schools have retained the word 'grammar' in their title even though the 11+ exam is no longer a requirement for entry, having been abolished in particular areas of the country.

HNC:
Higher National Certificate

Level 5 vocational qualification awarded by further and higher education providers.

HND:
Higher National Diploma

Level 5 vocational qualification awarded by further and higher education providers.

Horizontal grouping:

pupils organised into similar age groups for both subject teaching and form tutoring.

ICT:
Information Communication Technology

a broad range of communications technologies that will store, retrieve, manipulate, transmit or receive information electronically in a digital form.

IEP or ILP:
Individual Education/ Learning Plan

plan or programme compiled for pupils with particular learning needs.

Inclusion:

teaching approaches addressing the needs of pupils with a variety of backgrounds, abilities and needs.

Independent schools:

these schools lie outside government control and funding; they charge fees for pupils to attend the school and many operate an entrance exam system.

ITE:
Initial Teacher Education

the term used for the period of qualifying to become a teacher, usually involving school experiences and working towards Qualified Teacher Status (QTS).

Key stages:

In England the curriculum is divided into stages according to pupil age. Key Stage 1 relates to year groups 1 and 2 (ages 5–7). Key Stage 2 covers Years 3–6 (ages 7–11). Key Stage 3 is taught in the early years of secondary school, Years 7–9 (ages 11–14), although some secondary schools only follow Key Stage 3 in Years 7 and 8. Key Stage 4 is the GCSE years of 10 and 11, although some schools begin Key Stage 4 work in Year 9. Key Stage 5 relates to the post-16 curriculum.

LDO:
Leadership Development Officer

new 'Teach First' student teachers (see below) are assigned an LDO to support them through the training programme. These are usually teachers who have recently completed the Teach First pathway into teaching.

LSA:
Learning Support Assistant

LSAs work closely with teachers to support pupils in their learning. See also 'Support Staff'.

Maintained schools:

state schools that are 'maintained' by a local authority. These schools follow the national curriculum and national terms of employment for staff.

Mentor:

a named teacher with responsibility for supporting the learning and development of the student teacher.

Mentoring: *in the context of a school, the process by which an experienced teacher supports the learning and development of a student teacher.*

National curriculum: *a set of subjects and standards used by primary and secondary schools (although academies, free schools and independent schools do not have to follow the national curriculum).*

NCTL:
National College for Teaching and Leadership
currently allocates the number of teacher training places to accredited providers as well as performing a wider role in teacher and leadership development.

NQT:
Newly Qualified Teacher
The term used to describe teachers during their period of induction after being recommended for QTS. This period is normally one year for those working full time.

Ofsted:
The Office for Standards in Education, Children's Services and Skills
inspects and regulates services that care for children and young people, and services providing education and skills for learners of all ages.

Paradigm: *an example or model of an expected norm.*

Pastoral curriculum: *non-academic curriculum which addresses the well-being and safeguarding of pupils, including PSHE (see below).*

Pedagogy: *the principles and practice of teaching.*

Personalised learning: *learning which addresses the specific individual needs of the individual learner.*

PGCE:
Postgraduate Certificate in Education
*level 7 teaching qualification with a minimum of 40 credits at Masters level. Sometimes the acronym is shown as **PostGCE** (Postgraduate Certificate in Education) to distinguish it from the **ProfGCE** (Professional Graduate Certificate in Education) which is a level 6 qualification so does not have any Masters credits.*

PGDE:
Postgraduate Diploma in Education
some providers which award up to 120 credits at Masters level call the qualification a 'Diploma' in Education rather than a 'Certificate' in Education.

PPA:
Planning, Preparation and Assessment
10 per cent of a teacher's timetable is set aside for PPA. During the induction year PPA should account for 20 per cent of the timetable.

ProfGCE: *level 6 teaching qualification that is also generally called PGCE.*

Professional subject association: *subject organisations which support subject specialist teaching and learning, eg NATE (National Association for the Teaching of English); ASE (Association for Science Education); HA (Historical Association); GA (Geographical Association)*

Professional tutor: *generally a senior member of school staff with responsibility for working with mentors, NQTs and student teachers in the school.*

Progress 8:   *a means by which pupil progress and attainment are calculated using data from the same eight subjects from the end of primary school to the end of secondary education.*

PSHE:
Personal, Social,
Health and Economic
Education

aspects of the non-academic curriculum. In some schools this also includes Citizenship so the acronym may appear as PSHCE.

Pupil data: *a wide range of information kept about individual pupils that is used to monitor progress against predicted results.*

Pupil premium: *additional funding for schools to enable them to support pupils deemed to be at a disadvantage in order to raise their attainment from reception to Year 11. Schools which have pupils on the Free School Meals (FSM) register, and 'looked after' children (LAC) are eligible to receive this funding. Schools decide how the money will be spent.*

Pupil voice: *the views of pupils are sought and addressed through a school council or similar group.*

QTS:
Qualified Teacher Status

successful completion of a training pathway, where competence in the Teachers' Standards has been achieved, leads to the recommendation of QTS. After the successful completion of an induction year, with evidence of maintained competence in the Teachers' Standards, QTS is ratified. QTS is needed in order to work in a local authority school in England.

Reflection: *in the context of a school, this is the process by which teachers think through what they have done and review decisions and choices made before planning for future teaching.*

Reflexivity: *in the context of reflecting upon teaching episodes, the teacher's analysis of him/herself and the impact the 'self' has on the scenarios being reflected upon.*

Resilience: *the capacity to deal with the ongoing day-to-day challenge of working in a demanding role as well as specific challenging events.*

Safeguarding: *ensuring protection against danger, injury, etc (Collins English Dictionary).*

School council: *a body of elected representatives (usually teachers and pupils) who ensure that issues are raised and addressed before they become problems (Leibling and Prior, 2005).*

School Direct: *the pathway into teaching where you apply to a lead school to undertake your training.*

SCITT:
School-Centred Initial Teacher Training

a cluster of schools providing a training programme to award QTS.

SENCO:

Special Educational Needs Co-ordinator.

SEND:
Special Educational Needs and Disability

a general term referring to an extensive range of individual pupil learning needs.

SKE:
Subject Knowledge Enhancement

the term for courses run to provide extra subject knowledge beyond the QTS programme, usually but not exclusively before the PGCE/QTS programme commences.

Social media:

Facebook, Twitter, etc.

Subject pedagogy:

the principles and practices recommended for teaching a particular subject in school.

Subject tutor:

an individual subject specialist with responsibilities for monitoring and advising student teachers during their ITE.

Support staff:

people who offer additional support to teachers. They may be called Teaching Assistants (TAs) or Learning Support Assistants (LSAs). Other specialist staff may be available for specific support, eg educational psychologist, counsellor, dyslexia support, support for visually or hearing impaired pupils.

Teachers' Standards:

the national standards that define the skills and attributes expected of both student teachers and qualified teachers in England.

Teach First:

this is an educational charity recruiting high-achieving graduates to work in schools located in areas of economic deprivation where there is a local achievement gap between poorer children and their wealthier peers.

TEFL:

Teaching English as a Foreign Language.

TESOL:

Teaching English to Speakers of Other Languages.

UCAS:
Universities and Colleges Admissions Service

currently administers the application process for ITE courses; this process will be changing in 2017.

UTCs:
University Technical Colleges

these have been established to offer 14–18 year olds a curriculum focusing on technical and scientific subjects. Working in partnership with a local university and local employers, the aim is to develop scientists, engineers and technicians for future types of employment.

Vertical grouping:

pupils organised into mixed age groups for form tutoring. Subjects are rarely taught to mixed age groups.

Voluntary aided schools: *these are usually faith schools and the religious organisation is likely to own the land and buildings. The governing body employs the teaching staff and decides the school's admissions policy.*

Voluntary controlled schools: *these schools are run by the local authority which employs the teaching staff and sets the admissions policy.*

Well-being: *the condition of being contented, healthy or successful (Collins English Dictionary). In some schools 'happiness' is now a subject on the curriculum.*

REFERENCE

Leibling, M and Prior, R (2005) *The A-Z of Learning*. Abingdon: RoutledgeFalmer.

1 Introduction

Andy Davies and Mel Norman

This book is designed for anyone considering becoming a secondary teacher. The aim is to gain a 'warts and all' insight into the realities of such a choice, covering everything from the application process to the day-to-day realities of thriving as a secondary teacher. The writers of each chapter are all currently involved in a range of Initial Teacher Education (ITE) pathways and programmes, including undergraduate and postgraduate courses and different partnerships with a range of schools, following experience as successful secondary teachers. The information, ideas and advice are based upon their experience as teachers, teacher educators and researchers of teachers' professional learning in a wide variety of different settings. We should point out that, while advice contained in this book is relevant to readers interested in teaching in various contexts in all parts of the UK, the sections on policy and curriculum frameworks focus on England.

STRUCTURE AND CONTENT OF THE BOOK

The book is structured to help you to understand teaching and schools. Education, like any profession, is full of acronyms and technical language that can initially feel confusing and hard to understand. The *Jargon Buster* at the beginning of the book is a glossary of key terms used throughout this book, one which will give you the answer to many of the questions you may be too afraid to ask!

To help you to engage with the topics explored in Chapters 2–11 the following learning features are included.

- **Reflective tasks:** these are activities and questions designed to help you thoughtfully engage with the text. They will help you to better understand the topics and ultimately make up your mind about whether to get into secondary teaching.

- **Pupil / teacher / student voice:** these 'voice boxes' share the experiences of those involved in secondary teaching, helping to provide a rounded picture of the realities of learning to teach and working in secondary schools.

- **Research focus:** these summaries of important and influential research projects are designed to give you an informed and evidence-based understanding of different aspects of secondary teaching.

- **Progress checklist:** at the end of each chapter these sections summarise key points and help you to track your route towards a potential application for ITE.

○ **Taking it further:** here you are given resources to follow up on issues raised in each chapter. Books, blogs and other web links are included that give an accessible and deeper insight into the topics discussed.

In Chapter 2, Andy Davies and Tom Newlands help you to consider the question 'Is secondary teaching for me?' A range of views from student teachers, newly qualified teachers (NQTs) and more experienced practitioners are considered, alongside the voices of those who have decided that teaching is not for them. This is complemented by discussion of the differences between primary and secondary teaching. Common myths about secondary teaching are evaluated and contrasted with the realities, as evidenced by research and the accounts of those involved in teaching. Activities are presented that encourage personal reflection on the fundamental question of whether secondary teaching is for you and how you would address this in a potential application.

In Chapter 3, Paul Dickinson summarises and clarifies the different pathways you can choose to follow to become a secondary teacher. He presents an overview of the core elements that are likely to exist in any of these pathways and explains the key differences between them to help you select the right route for you. This chapter situates current pathways within the context of recent government policy in England, including the growth of school-based pathways such as School Direct. Comments from current students and qualified teachers about the particular routes they have chosen are highlighted in order to provide a sense of what factors recent applicants have considered when applying for their chosen pathway and how they subsequently feel about those decisions.

In Chapter 4, Mel Norman explores current education policy and its impact on secondary teachers and their working lives. Current policy priorities are discussed and the impact of policy reforms on teachers and those learning to teach are highlighted. Policy changes to the curriculum, public examinations and teacher professionalism are addressed as well as the significant, and not always welcome, influence of Ofsted. The chapter also discusses the diverse nature of schools and offers you an opportunity to reflect on the challenges of working in a different school environment, including free schools, academies, faith schools, grammar schools and maintained schools, and what each of these offer both pupils and teachers.

In Chapter 5, Gary Stidder and Andy Davies focus on the nature of professional learning as a teacher. The processes and challenges of qualifying as a secondary teacher are framed by an investigation of the current (at the time of writing) Teachers' Standards (DfE, 2013) that need to be met to achieve Qualified Teacher Status (QTS). You are guided through the demands of these Teachers' Standards from the perspectives of recently qualified teachers, who discuss challenges and the strategies they have used to overcome them. The importance of a rounded experience in learning to be a teacher is also explored so that the place and purpose of the academic study of education is discussed and explained, including how and why theory and assignment writing relate to practical school-based work. Finally, there is a focus on the role of subject mentor support for student teachers and other aspects of the school placement experience, including workload management.

In Chapter 6, Brian Marsh and Chris Sweeney discuss the importance of subject knowledge and expertise in secondary education. The need to have a passion for a subject specialism and the ability to inspire the same in others is described as being at the heart of effective secondary teaching. The importance for teachers to continually develop and enhance their understanding of subject knowledge and the ability to develop understanding of that subject in others is the chapter's key theme. This is supported by the voices of new and more experienced teachers discussing how they engage with such challenges.

In Chapter 7, Sally Johnson and Sarah Poore focus on the demands of classroom practice. This gives you an insight into school life from the point of view of the different parties involved: school staff, ITE tutors, pupils and parents. The chapter considers the strategies teachers use to maintain their well-being and to deal with the stresses, strains and also the benefits of working in schools. Classroom practice is explored by considering the challenges of behaviour management and developing an inclusive learning environment. There is also discussion of the challenges of working with different groups of learners and the ways in which teachers support the progress of all pupils through strategies such as differentiation and the monitoring of progress data.

In Chapter 8, Karen Murray-Hall and Mel Norman focus on the main challenges of working with secondary school age pupils. The chapter explores the great responsibilities teachers face as role models and how supporting young people goes beyond the remit of being a subject specialist. This role encompasses the well-being and development of every pupil beyond the academic; it involves the development of the child as a person, not just as a pupil. This can include responsibility for personal, social, health and economic education (PSHE), dealing with individual pupil issues, home-school liaison and safeguarding. The voices of pupils and the teachers who work with them are presented to give a rounded picture of the realities of working with young people.

In Chapter 9, Nickey Brown and Mark Boylan address what is needed to thrive as a teacher. This chapter considers the skills, attributes and dispositions needed to be a successful teacher in the profession today. The chapter encourages you to engage in reflective exercises to examine different metaphors for teaching and to self-reflect on your strengths and qualities in relation to these and how they link to your values and aims as a teacher. Models of resilience are discussed and readers are encouraged to develop strategies for self-care to support their well-being to thrive as a teacher both during ITE and throughout their careers.

In Chapter 10, Bhavna Prajapat and Steve Roberts guide you through the entire ITE application process from choosing a pathway to completing a written application before giving advice on what to expect in a formal interview. There is consideration of how to learn from school visits before an interview, how to identify what your training needs are and how to find out about different providers that suit your preferences. Advice on the application process provided in this chapter draws upon particular insights from the range of professionals typically involved in admissions and reflects on the particular role each plays in making the decisions to: a) invite the applicant to interview; and b) offer a place on the course to the successful applicant. The chapter also discusses the range and variety of possible tasks and challenges that different subject pathways and different provider institutions may set as requirements for the interview process, as well as providing guidance on passing the literacy and numeracy Skills Tests. The chapter gives you guidance on how to request feedback following unsuccessful interviews, and concludes on the more positive note of how successful applicants can maintain and develop their relationship with the chosen provider after accepting an offer of a place on their course.

The conclusion of this book identifies and summarises key themes discussed in the preceding chapters. It continues by considering secondary teaching in the contemporary context, discussing current employment prospects and the importance of engaging in continuing professional development before discussing how current reforms are likely to impact on secondary education.

REFERENCE

Department for Education (DfE) (2013) *Teachers' Standards: Guidance for School Leaders, School Staff and Governing Bodies (Introduction updated June 2013).* London: Department for Education.

2 Is secondary teaching for you?

Andy Davies and Tom Newlands

INTRODUCTION

The aim of this chapter is to support you in making an informed decision about whether or not to apply to become a secondary teacher. We wouldn't be contributing to this book and writing the chapter unless we believed that teaching is a worthwhile, challenging and rewarding choice of career, but we are keenly aware that it is not for everyone. This chapter enables you to engage with a range of views from student teachers, more experienced practitioners, admissions tutors and those who have left the profession, as well as findings from relevant research projects. Reflective activities are presented to support you in considering crucial questions about whether secondary teaching is for you. These are drawn together in the progress checklist later in this chapter. While we seek to provide a rounded view of what secondary teaching is like, this chapter should be read in conjunction with observation visits to secondary schools and conversations with practising teachers. The importance of these visits and conversations cannot be overemphasised. It would be unwise to make such a life-changing decision without them.

As a secondary teacher you would be joining a large profession of talented and dedicated individuals. Currently in England there are an estimated 213,000 secondary teachers working in 3000 state schools and academies responsible for around 3 million pupils (DfE, 2014a). Rates of employment for Newly Qualified Teachers (NQTs) are excellent, with 94 per cent of secondary NQTs reported as being in employment after finishing their ITE in 2013 (DfE/NCTL, 2014).

This is a profession that welcomes people with a range of skills and attributes from a variety of backgrounds and at different stages of their lives. Among the characteristics of those undertaking secondary ITE in 2013:

o   *96 per cent followed a postgraduate route into teaching;*

o   *63 per cent were female;*

o   *16 per cent were from ethnic minority groups;*

o   *53 per cent were 25 years of age or older.*

(Smithers et al, 2013)

The choice of career of a secondary teacher works for a lot of different people, but it is still a decision that should not be taken lightly.

> ### Reflective task
>
> As you read this chapter you should critically reflect on and analyse the reasons you have for considering teaching as a career. As a starting point, note down your initial answers to the following questions.
>
> o   Why are you considering teaching?
>
> o   Why are you considering teaching in secondary schools?
>
> o   Why do you want to teach a specific subject?

WHY TEACH?

The question 'Is secondary teaching for you?' is one of many serious questions that you may be asking yourself. Others may be:

o   Why am I considering teaching?

o   Do I have the skills to be a secondary teacher?

o   Am I resilient enough to deal with the challenges of working in a secondary school?

However, before you think about secondary teaching more specifically you will have thought – or else need to think – about why you want to teach in general.

'Why teach?' is a question you will certainly need to address on your application forms and at interviews, whichever pathway into teaching you take. Answers to this question are varied and underlying these are motivations, ideals and values that say something about you and your potential teacher identity. It is not a question that you should be asking only at this point but one that you should revisit throughout your teaching career, as part of being a critically reflective practitioner.

Your decision about whether to teach or not, your choice of primary or secondary teaching and your proposed subject specialism will be related to and shaped by your experiences in education and beyond. Your prior life experience is unique and you can use this to bring something valuable and different to teaching.

Why secondary teaching?

In making the choice to become a secondary teacher it is important to reflect on the similarities and differences between primary and secondary schools and what it is that potentially attracts you to the latter. Table 2.1 compares characteristics of primary and secondary schools.

It may be that you feel you can relate more to an older age group and look forward to the challenge of teaching adolescents, in what are very formative years. One of the main reasons for choosing secondary teaching is a passion or enthusiasm for a particular subject. This may be a subject that you enjoyed at school, was taught well and then

Table 2.1 Characteristics of primary and secondary schools

	Primary	**Secondary**
Number of schools in England	16,788	3329
Age range	4 to 11 years old	11 to 18 years old
Average size of school	263 pupils	956 pupils
Specialist subjects	All subjects in the national curriculum at a 'sound, basic' level	One or two subjects from the national curriculum
Working part-time	27.9%	18.8%
Average salary	£35,800	£36,600
Male / female teaching staff	65,000 (9%) / 681,000 (91%)	132,000 (29%) / 317,500 (71%)

Sources: DfE (2014c, 2014d and 2014e)

chose to study at university, though not necessarily. Furthermore, other reasons may be the challenge of inspiring a love of a subject in pupils, the opportunity to focus on it at GCSE and even A level and a philosophical commitment to the value of the subject in the secondary education of the whole child. Compared to primary teaching there is less contact time with the pupils you teach; more pupils will be taught per week and you will work with a range of year groups rather than one, and this variety may appeal to you.

Tim trained to be a primary school teacher, working in that setting for ten years before undertaking a two-year secondment in a secondary school as an English teacher. He provides insights into the nature of these two phases.

Teacher voice

Tim's view: how is secondary teaching different from primary teaching?

Fundamentally, the values of a teacher are the same in both – it is about educating the children. However, you are dealing with children and young people at different stages of their lives with different needs and views of themselves and the world. One of the challenges of secondary teaching is the teacher-pupil relationship. Primary school teachers, because they have so much more time with the pupils, get to know them in so much more depth. Although good secondary teachers also do that it is a different sort of relationship.

I suppose one of the differences is around the depth of subject knowledge required at secondary level. What is similar though is the ability to take that subject knowledge and make it engaging and challenging for young people. Primary school teachers are more in charge of the way the day is structured – I could decide when literacy or numeracy was in the day. There is something about the high stakes of exams as well – GCSE, A level. This means that there is a potential for education to be too exam-focused. There tend to be more opportunities for career progression in a secondary school as these are very different organisations to primary schools.

The broader context

The questions 'Why teach?' and 'Why secondary teaching?' can be asked at a personal level but should also be considered within the broader political and social context. The central importance of education for a country's well-being and economic prospects means that schooling is a topic of national significance. Education is a key part of every government's agenda, meaning that the nature of the job and the day-to-day experiences of teachers are subject to continual change as new governments come to power. Ongoing change is a feature of every teaching career. Furthermore, images of secondary education in the media do not always paint a positive picture of the profession with, for example, news of pay negotiations, industrial action, teacher disillusionment and resignations. It is therefore important to familiarise yourself with the nature of secondary teaching in order to decide whether or not it is for you.

WHAT IS IT LIKE BEING A SECONDARY TEACHER?

Trying to present a picture of what being a secondary teacher is like is difficult.

○ Firstly, there is a diverse range of schools (eg maintained schools, academies, free schools, faith schools) with different principles, priorities and curricula. This is a diversity that is increasing as education reforms are encouraging innovation to support pupil progress (see Chapter 4 – 'Secondary teaching today').

○ Secondly, there are wide differences between subject areas related to their status and place in each school.

○ Thirdly, the uniqueness of every individual pupil means that classes are varied, as are the resulting challenges to teachers.

This section presents different perspectives on the question of what it is like to be a secondary teacher but should be read with the understanding that (as noted above) there is considerable diversity beyond that presented here.

Expectations of teachers

A good starting point to gain an insight into the nature of the job is the Teachers' Standards (DfE, 2013) that define the *'minimum level of practice expected of trainees and teachers*' (p 2). Demonstrating competence in relation to these standards enables student teachers to gain Qualified Teacher Status (QTS). These standards cover both primary and secondary teaching, characterising eight areas of teaching and describing the expectations for personal and professional conduct. The Teachers' Standards form the focus of work during ITE and are used to judge the competence and progress of qualified professionals. The Teachers' Standards (DfE, 2013) can be found easily online. Developing an understanding of them will be beneficial in preparing for the application and interview process. Further discussion of the Teachers' Standards can be found in Chapter 5 – Professional learning as a secondary teacher.

Reflective task

Read the Teachers' Standards (DfE, 2013) and note your responses to the following questions.

○ What prior experiences and skills do you have that might support you in meeting these standards?

○ What areas will you most need to develop in order to meet these standards?

Subject specialism

Secondary teachers are united by the need to hold a subject specialism in which they possess a depth of knowledge and a professional understanding of how to teach and inspire pupils in that area. As a rule, secondary teachers' specialist areas relate to the national curriculum (English, mathematics, science subjects, design and technology, computing, foreign languages, music, history, geography and physical education). Other subjects are also taught – religious education and PSHE. While these are not statutory subjects in the national curriculum, they are perceived as core parts of the broader '*social, moral, spiritual and cultural*' development of young people (Ofsted, 2012).

In your specialism you will need to be able to demonstrate the requisite subject know-ledge and a desire to develop it. Most pathways into teaching require you to hold a relevant degree, although it can be from a related area. For example, the Department for Education website (DfE, 2014c) advises that to teach mathematics you could hold a degree in the areas of economics, statistics, accountancy or engineering, instead of mathematics itself. For some subject areas there are opportunities to develop subject knowledge prior to or after application through following Subject Knowledge Enhancement or bridging courses (see Chapter 6 for further details). There are also some undergraduate routes into secondary teaching in which a subject specialism is studied to degree level at the same time as undertaking school experience.

Secondary schools

While differences exist between schools there are typical features in terms of the struc-ture, staffing, calendar and timetable.

- **Structure**: Typically secondary schools include pupils from the ages of 11 to 16 or 18. Normally there is a clear hierarchy with a governing body and a headteacher (or principal), supported by deputies and assistants. Most commonly the organisation will be structured to support pupils pastorally (relating to their welfare) and academically (associated with learning and attainment).

- **Teaching staff**: As a new teacher you will normally join a departmental team. Subject teachers tend to work together as a team to plan, collaborate and support one another. You will also become part of a wider teaching staff, often including heads of year, heads of department and form tutors (although the names and scope of these roles vary widely).

- **Support staff**: The wider team in a school will include a variety of colleagues who you will collaborate with. These include teaching assistants, administrative staff and other professionals, such as educational psychologists, who may work in a number of different schools.

- **The calendar**: Different schools are increasingly varying the organisation of the academic year although currently most schools still follow a three-term year. Typically these terms run from September to December (autumn term), January to March (spring term) and April to July (summer term), with holidays in between. All schools must be open for 190 days a year with teachers contracted to a minimum of another five days for in-service education and training (INSET) days.

- **The timetable**: Timetables are decided by the individual school's governing body, and normally work on a one-week or two-week cycle with a number of slots for lessons per day. As well as teaching time, teachers receive a number of preparation, planning and assessment (PPA) periods, usually accounting for 10 per cent of their overall timetable (NASUWT, 2014).

The following experiences of three teachers at different stages of their careers provide an insight into day-to-day life as a secondary teacher. Sarah is an assistant principal at an 11–16 academy; Anwar is a head of history and politics, and Camilla is a teacher of PSHE and psychology, both at 11–18 schools.

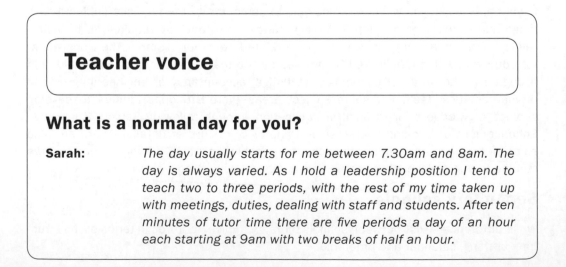

Teacher voice

What is a normal day for you?

Sarah: *The day usually starts for me between 7.30am and 8am. The day is always varied. As I hold a leadership position I tend to teach two to three periods, with the rest of my time taken up with meetings, duties, dealing with staff and students. After ten minutes of tutor time there are five periods a day of an hour each starting at 9am with two breaks of half an hour.*

Anwar:	*Busy! I get the 6.50am train and start work then – using the journey to mark. I usually arrive at 8am and before classes start catch up with admin, speak to colleagues, get lessons ready, respond to emails and meet pupils. I tend to teach five out of six lessons each day with a 15-minute break and a half-hour lunch. Non-teaching periods usually involve 'one to ones' with pupils or other teachers. The school day normally ends at 4.15pm but on Wednesdays we finish teaching an hour early for meetings. I invariably work three evenings out of five and, most weeks, six hours on a Sunday.*
Camilla:	*We start at 8.35am with registration or assembly and then have five hour-long lessons with two breaks (morning 25 minutes and lunchtime 35 minutes) and finish by 3pm. On Tuesdays and Thursdays we hold enrichment sessions from 3pm to 4pm which all pupils can opt to follow. There is never a day that's the same because you are dealing with different people all the time.*

Secondary teaching: fact and fiction

As virtually every adult will have been through secondary education they are all in some way an 'expert' in it, or at least they think they are! Strong opinions are held regarding teachers and schooling that are often repeated as if commonly known facts, which actually deserve to be challenged. The following common examples illustrate how myths and misconceptions can be perpetuated.

Misconception 1: 'It's all summer holidays and home at 3pm'

It is normal for schools to have generous breaks between terms – 12 weeks a year is standard – and to finish whole-class teaching between 3 and 4pm. However, as Anwar suggested above, this does not mean that teaching equates to a part-time job. Figures from the Department for Education (DfE, 2014b) suggest that secondary teachers on average work 55 hours a week, with 19 hours timetabled for teaching. The rest of their time is spent planning, preparing, marking, providing general pastoral and academic support for pupils, and carrying out administrative tasks. It is also standard practice for teachers to work during part of their holidays in order to prepare for the following term.

Misconception 2: 'The pay is terrible'

There is a commonly held misconception that teachers receive lower pay than comparable professionals. Currently starting pay is actually considered high compared to other graduates in England, and from an international perspective experienced teachers' pay is in line with other western European countries (House of Commons Education Committee, 2012). Minimum salaries start at just over £20,000 and can rise as high as six figures for headteachers (DfE, 2014c). Recent reforms such as the introduction of performance-related pay mean that schools can establish their own salary structure in an attempt to attract and reward those they see as the best teachers.

Misconception 3: 'Those who can, do; those who can't, teach'

This is a commonly heard put-down of teachers, suggesting that teaching is an easy choice of profession, and a refuge for people who have failed elsewhere. Considering the complex nature of teaching and learning, as well as the challenges of working with young people on a daily basis, this does not reflect the reality of the professionalism, dedication and skills of the vast majority of those who work in schools.

Career paths

You would probably start as a classroom teacher but you could later decide to apply for promotion, taking on a role such as head of year or head of department with increased responsibility and pay. Career progression in teaching can take very different forms, ranging from classroom roles to more managerial positions. Below are accounts by Sarah, Anwar and Camilla, who we heard from before, regarding their career paths.

Teacher voice

Career progression

Sarah: *My first role was as a classroom teacher, before becoming head of drama 12 months later. Another year on I became head of the creative arts faculty, overseeing drama, art and music. Then later I became an advanced skills teacher for drama, a role which saw me supporting other schools and teachers. Two years on I became an assistant head. I then worked part-time as an advanced skills teacher while my two children were young. Then I returned to my previous post as assistant head, a post that I hold to the present day.*

Anwar: *I started as a main scale history teacher and then applied to become head of PSHE / citizenship, which was great. I also took on acting head of politics for a maternity cover, all at the same school. I then moved school to become head of history. I need to now think whether to push on or stick. I love being in the classroom the most but am aware the time might be coming to try and move upwards!*

Camilla: *I did my training in South Africa with three months' worth of teaching practice but my main experience has been in the*

English system. I have been teaching for eight years and have taught food technology, then English, then drama. I went to a second school after about two years and started teaching PSHE. I was there for three years and came over to my current school as there was a position open for a psychology and PSHE teacher.

Career opportunities beyond the classroom

Many people work successfully as teachers for a number of years, making a substantial contribution to pupil learning, before moving into other related areas of employment. Working as a teacher equips you with skills and experiences that can support you in a range of other jobs, such as:

○ an adviser or consultant to teachers in schools in your specialist subject;

○ an educational specialist such as a speech therapist or educational psychologist (normally requires further training and study);

○ an educational officer for museums, charities or arts organisations;

○ an educational researcher (normally requires successful completion of a doctorate).

WHAT PUTS PEOPLE OFF BEING A SECONDARY TEACHER?

At different stages many people decide that teaching is not for them; some without applying to a teaching programme, some during or at the end of their ITE and others during or at the end of their NQT induction or after working as a fully qualified teacher. While more than nine out of ten teachers in England say they actually enjoy the job (Ratcliffe, 2014), an estimated two-fifths of teachers still leave the profession within five years of qualifying (Wilshaw, 2014), although this is a contentious statistic because many of these individuals are believed to return at a later date.

Research focus

Cockburn, A and Hadyn, T (2004) *Recruiting and Retaining Teachers: Understanding Why Teachers Teach*. London: Routledge.

This work suggests that potential applicants are most commonly put off from applying to teach for the following reasons:

○ stress;

○ pupil behaviour and discipline;

○ workload.

Their research suggests that these factors are pretty well-founded as the top four reasons for those considering leaving teaching are:

1. workload;

2. work-life balance;

3. stress / exhaustion;

4. pupil behaviour and discipline.

Another recent survey reported in *The Guardian* suggested that the high number of new government initiatives was the most significant factor identified by those considering leaving the profession in 2011 (Berliner, 2011). These pressures, commonly associated with Ofsted and a 'target-driven culture', have been identified as problematic by both teachers and their unions (Paton, 2013). It is certainly worth considering how you will engage with such challenges and what prior experience and skills you could draw upon to do so.

The voices of three individuals who decided not to teach are presented below. Oliver left during his PGCE, Anya taught for five years as a science teacher and Cathie taught for 17 years as a secondary languages teacher.

Teacher voice

Reasons for not being a secondary teacher

Oliver: *Despite feeling enthusiastic about the challenge and the prospect of pursuing a career which I believed was honourable and rewarding, I was not prepared for the level of personal sacrifice required to be successful. During this process I found very little gratification or satisfying moments that might have given me the boost to carry on, while feeling increasingly unhealthy and unhappy due to the time-consuming nature of the task. The teaching profession has been under a lot of strain lately, and this can certainly be felt on the front line, within schools. There is no doubt that this negative atmosphere can be felt as a student teacher.*

Anya: *There are a few reasons I left teaching ... I returned from maternity leave to the school and found it difficult to balance being a parent with the timetable and workload of being a secondary teacher. I found the management increasingly unsympathetic* *and it became impossible to carry on. I cannot confidently attribute it to teaching per se rather the culture in teaching and the culture in the school. I definitely feel working where I did was a traumatic experience and the impact has been far-reaching – even thinking about it now I feel a rising sense of tension.*

Cathie: *I am leaving teaching after 17 years with a heavy heart. Why? Workload. We are overburdened with collecting data, writing individual lesson plans to meet the needs of every pupil and then give up lunchtimes and breaks to get pupils to meet targets that often they don't care about. Don't get me wrong, it is important to meet all pupils' needs and to help them fulfil their potential but the pressure of league tables means that we work twice as hard as the pupils because they can't fail. We don't really teach them about responsibility and perseverance, for all the buzz words we are required to use.*

Reflective task

Having read through these accounts of individuals choosing not to enter or remain in the profession, consider how you might respond to these challenges.

o   How might you seek to overcome or avoid challenges such as these?

o   What else, if anything, might be putting you off becoming a secondary teacher, and how much of an issue do you think this is?

In considering the accounts of these individuals and the reasons they give for leaving or not entering teaching, it is important to acknowledge that teaching is certainly not an easy option. It is important, however, to remember that while there are some generic issues that teachers can find difficult, the factors putting some teachers off the profession often (but not always) develop from individual school environments and professional relationships, so giving careful thought to the choice of school in which you will work (to the extent that you are able to choose) is of the utmost importance.

WHAT IS GOOD ABOUT BEING A SECONDARY TEACHER?

After considering the reasons why people choose to leave the profession, you should also explore what secondary teachers like about their job.

Research focus

Hobson, A, Malderez, A, Tracey, L, Homer, M, Ashby, P, Mitchell, N, McIntyre, J, Cooper, D, Roper, T, Chambers, G and Tomlinson, P (2009) *Becoming a Teacher: Teachers' Experiences of Initial Teacher Training, Induction and Early Professional Development – Final Report*. Nottingham: University of Nottingham and Department for Children, Schools and Families.

Hobson et al conducted a survey of 4790 student teachers, subsequently tracking their experiences and perspectives over five years. As NQTs they were asked whether they enjoyed teaching, and 93 per cent said they did. The following three areas were identified as the most common high points of their first year:

1. good relationships with pupils;

2. perception of pupil learning and their role in bringing this about;

3. good relationships with colleagues.

Teacher voice

What do you like about being a secondary teacher?

Sarah: *The best part of my job is the pupils. That may sound like a cliché, but it is true. Seeing pupils succeed and achieving their goals is incredibly rewarding. Each day and each class can be different, but they all have an equal measure of laughter, frustration (sometimes) and surprise, which keeps you motivated and means you are never bored!*

Anwar: *The list is virtually endless! But in essence the best things are:*

1. *Inspiring the pupils*

2. *The creativity involved*

3. *The lack of boredom*

4. *Subject matter – I love history and politics*

5. *The cyclical nature of the year. I think the pattern of intense work and then holidays suits my personality*

6. *Cool colleagues – I know teachers can moan but they are generally really lovely people who have gone into the profession for pretty altruistic reasons.*

7. *The foreign travel. This has been a total unexpected bonus of teaching but (if you are prepared to organise the trips) it can be incredible.*

Camilla: *I like being in a school where I can be part of the community, where I can get really involved. I want to love my job. And I do love it, it really is fascinating. That said, some days I actually hate it but most of the time it's incredible!*

BRINGING IT TOGETHER

Multiple and complex reasons

Wanting to teach is based on multiple, complex personal reasons and experiences. One survey of student teachers suggests there is a range of reasons that include:

○ *family tradition;*

○ *inspirational teachers;*

○ *love of a subject;*

○ *the influence of friends;*

○ *a sense of vocation;*

○ *a desire to change career;*

○ *a reaction to poor teaching.*

(Lamb, 2006, p 16)

Other research supports the view that it is not always positive reasons that lead someone to choose teaching:

remembered experiences of unhelpful and barely competent teachers have spurred some individuals on to represent their field of expertise more successfully, as if to undo the faults of predecessors.

(Gordon, 2006, p 4)

It may be that you feel you were taught by a poor teacher in a particular subject at school or you did not receive the support you needed to progress. A student of ours said she was keen to 'ensure that young people are given opportunities to learn' that she 'didn't have at school'.

Student teacher voice

What else do secondary student teachers say about their reasons for wanting to teach?

- ○ *I wanted to do a job where I had the chance to have a positive impact on other people's lives.*
- ○ *I wanted to do something productive and meaningful with my degree.*
- ○ *I wanted to give young people the same opportunities I had.*
- ○ *I like working with and have an affinity with young people.*
- ○ *I had worked as a teaching assistant.*
- ○ *I wanted to make social change.*
- ○ *It suited my skills.*
- ○ *To see and create 'penny dropping' and inspirational moments.*
- ○ *To have a career where every day is different and every day something makes you laugh.*
- ○ *I wanted job satisfaction and security.*
- ○ *The structure of the year and long holidays.*
- ○ *Career progression opportunities.*

Reflective task

Reflecting on the reasons identified by Lamb (2006) and those from the student teachers quoted above, consider the following questions.

- ○ Do you relate personally to any of these reasons and if so in what ways?
- ○ Do any of the reasons surprise you and why? Might you challenge any?

Research focus

Intrinsic and extrinsic motivations

Farkas, S, Johnson, J and Foleno, T (2000) *A Sense of Calling: Who Teaches and Why*. New York: Public Agenda.

It is possible to categorise motivations for wanting to teach as being either intrinsic or extrinsic. In a survey of what inspired new teachers to join the profession, Farkas et al (2000) identified examples of both intrinsic factors (eg *'teaching is work I love to do'*) and also extrinsic ones (eg *'teaching has job security'*). After analysing their data their conclusion suggested intrinsic rather than extrinsic factors were far more powerful in inspiring new teachers, who they characterised as *'looking to do work out of love rather than money'* (p 10).

Reflective task

○ Consider and then outline your own reasons for wanting to teach.

○ Are intrinsic or extrinsic motivations more powerful for you?

APPLICATIONS AND INTERVIEWS

In applications and at interview you will undoubtedly need to address the two questions 'Why teach?' and 'Why secondary teaching?' What you say may provoke a range of responses, both positive and negative. A number of secondary admissions tutors were asked to comment on which answers to the above two questions they like and dislike hearing from applicants to ITE programmes.

	Why teach?	Why secondary teaching?
Like to hear	*'I am committed to pupil development, education and my subject, in that order. The reasons being ...'* Carefully considered (and succinct) personal narratives that show awareness of teaching as a potentially rewarding and fulfilling career that is mostly about working with young people for their benefit and development – particularly expressed through subject-specific language (*'the advantages of a positive experience of education in this subject are ...'*). Reasons based on the experience of visiting a school or working with children and an informed view of what secondary schools are like.	*'I am passionate about my subject and want the subject to be the focus of my work – in a primary school you have to be an 'expert' in all subjects, which is impossible.'* Thoughtful awareness of specific characteristics of the 11–18 age range and differences within that range, and enthusiasm. Humour for dealing with the challenges of working with young people and teenagers. It is generally better to show rather than tell when it comes to enthusiasm for your subject.

Do not like to hear	'Can't think of anything else to do with my degree.'	'Don't like primary age children' / 'can't teach my higher subject knowledge to primary age children'.
	'Seems like a good idea now I've finished my degree.'	'I can have a better conversation with teenagers than children' / 'I don't want to teach the basics' (ie ill-informed and dismissive views of primary teaching).
	'It will fit in with having a family as the holidays are long!'	
	'It runs in the family.'	
	Reasons such as 'want to make a difference / give something back / pass on my knowledge / share my love of the subject' are vague, impersonal clichés! They need to be reinforced with personal examples and a concrete reference to teaching.	'I really only want to teach A level.'
		Discuss the appeal of teaching in general and not specifically secondary teaching.
		Anything that shows lack of consideration and lack of depth and commitment.
	Overt cynicism in jokey responses about an easy life or long holidays.	No experience of working with children or observing in a secondary school informing applicants' choice/answer.

Clearly, not all admissions tutors have the same preferences so there is not going to be one magic formula for you to repeat. However, it is worth thinking very carefully about your responses to these questions and what you are communicating about yourself and your philosophy of education in the answers that you give. In thinking about secondary teaching you are hopefully declaring a commitment to pupils, education and your chosen subject. See Chapter 10 – 'Successfully applying for a secondary ITE place' for further information and advice.

CONCLUSION

The aim of this chapter was to help you to make an informed decision about whether or not to apply to become a secondary teacher. Based on a range of evidence, this chapter has sought to support you in a potentially life-changing decision. You should now be more aware of what skills and attributes you will need to demonstrate and the areas for further investigation.

The next section presents a progress checklist that can be used to draw together the reflective tasks and support preparation for the application and interview process. This is then followed by 'Taking it Further', which presents key readings that provide additional evidence and perspectives related to the content of this chapter.

✓ # Progress checklist

Reflective tasks

As you read this chapter we asked you to complete five reflective tasks designed to support you in the decision about whether to apply to teach. By engaging in these tasks you will have considered the following:

○ your motivation for teaching a particular subject as a secondary teacher;

○ the skills and experiences you might be able to bring to bear as a teacher;

○ how you might respond to the challenges that you could face as a teacher.

Having now read this chapter and completed the reflective tasks, you should once again address the central question 'Is secondary teaching for you?'

It will be a good idea to keep hold of this provisional answer, which you may refine further as you read the other chapters in this book. Furthermore, you may be able to use it as part of your personal statement on an application form and/or in interviews.

Next steps

In order to present a rounded view of what it is like being a secondary teacher, we strongly recommend (if you haven't already done so) that you gain experience of secondary teaching by organising visits to a school and observing lessons in the subject area you are interested in. It is a common expectation of candidates attending interviews that they have engaged in such an experience, so schools are used to receiving such requests.

▶▶ **TAKING IT FURTHER**

Ellis, V (2013) *Learning and Teaching in the Secondary School.* 5th ed. London: Sage.

Provides guidance for student teachers on the professional skills, attributes and knowledge needed during ITE.

Hobson, A J, Malderez, A and Tracey, L (2009) *Navigating Initial Teacher Training: Becoming a Teacher.* London: Routledge.

Based on the experience of thousands of beginner teachers, this book provides support for those undertaking ITE and becoming a teacher.

The following article from the same research deals specifically with the experience of becoming and being a student teacher:

Malderez, A, Hobson, A J, Tracey, L and Kerr, K (2007). Becoming a Student Teacher: Core Features of the Experience. *European Journal of Teacher Education*, 30(3): 225–48.

About teaching

Department for Education: Get into Teaching website. www.education. gov.uk/get-into-teaching (accessed 30 July 2015).

This website provides guidance on pay and conditions as well as accounts by students and teachers describing their experiences of working in secondary schools.

Blogs and twitter feeds

There are many excellent blogs and twitter feeds written by teachers that give a real insight into the nature of the job. A few good starting points are:

Andrew Old: http://teachingbattleground.wordpress.com/ (accessed 30 July 2015)

Laura McInerney: http://lauramcinerney.com/ (accessed 30 July 2015)

Martin Said: @saidthemac

Teacher Toolkit: @Teachertoolkit

REFERENCES

Berliner, W (2011) I love teaching but ... *The Guardian*, 3 October 2011. [online] Available at: www.theguardian.com/teacher-network/teacher-blog/2011/oct/03/i-love-teaching-but (accessed 21 August 2014).

Cockburn, A and Hadyn, T (2004) *Recruiting and Retaining Teachers: Understanding Why Teachers Teach*. London: Routledge.

Department for Education (DfE) (2013) *Teachers Standards: Guidance for School Leaders, School Staff and Governing Bodies (Introduction updated June 2013)*. London: Department for Education.

Department for Education (DfE) (2014a) *School Workforce in England, November 2013, Statistical First Release 11/2014*. London: Department for Education.

Department for Education (DfE) (2014b) *Teachers' Workload Diary Survey 2013, Research Report 316*. London: Department for Education.

Department for Education (DfE) (2014c) *Get into Teaching – Teacher Salaries*. [online] Available at: www.education.gov.uk/get-into-teaching/about-teaching/salary (accessed 28 August 2014).

Department for Education (DfE) (2014d) *Statistical First Release: Schools and their Characteristics: January 2014*. [online] Available at: www.gov.uk/government/uploads/system/uploads/attachment_data/file/335176/2014_SPC_SFR_Text_v101.pdf (accessed 21 October 2014).

Department for Education (DfE) (2014e) *School Workforce in England: November 2013*. [online] Available at: www.gov.uk/government/statistics/school-workforce-in-england-november-2013 (accessed 31 October 2014).

Department for Education (DfE)/NCTL (2014) *Newly Qualified Teachers: Annual Survey 2013, Research Report 306*. London: Department for Education / National College for Teaching and Leadership.

Farkas, S, Johnson, J and Foleno, T (2000) *A Sense of Calling: Who Teaches and Why*. New York: Public Agenda.

Gordon, J (2006) Introduction, in Battersby, J and Gordon, J (eds) *Preparing to Teach: Learning from Experience*. Abingdon: Routledge.

Hobson, A, Malderez, A, Tracey, L, Homer, M, Ashby, P, Mitchell, N, McIntyre, J, Cooper, D, Roper, T, Chambers, G and Tomlinson, P (2009) *Becoming a Teacher: Teachers' Experiences of Initial Teacher Training, Induction and Early Professional Development: Final Report*. Nottingham: University of Nottingham and Department for Children, Schools and Families.

House of Commons Education Committee (2012) *Great Teachers: Attracting, Training and Retaining the Best (Ninth Report of the Session 2010–12)*. London: The Stationery Office Limited.

Lamb, P (2006) Wanting to Teach, in Battersby, J and Gordon, J (eds) *Preparing to Teach: Learning from Experience*. Abingdon: Routledge.

NASUWT (2014) *Directed Time in England, National Association of Schoolmasters Union of Women Teachers*. [online] Available at: www.nasuwt.org.uk/JoinNASUWT/AboutNASUWT/AboutNASUWT/index.htm (accessed 17 October 2014).

Ofsted (2012) *Good Practice Resource – Raising Achievement by Promoting Outstanding Spiritual, Moral, Social and Cultural Development*. London: Office for Standards in Education, Children's Services and Skills.

Paton, G (2013) Teachers call for boycotts of school Ofsted inspections, *The Telegraph*, 30 March 2013. [online] Available at: www.telegraph.co.uk/education/educationnews/9962568/Teachers-call-for-boycott-of-school-Ofsted-inspections.html (accessed 1 November 2014).

Ratcliffe, R (2014) A third of teachers would consider an alternative career, *The Guardian*, 29 April 2014. [online] Available at: www.theguardian.com/teacher-network/teacher-blog/2014/apr/29/teachers-alternative-careers-school-recruitment (accessed 28 August 2014).

Smithers, A, Robinson, P and Coughlan, M (2013) *The Good Teacher Training Guide 2013*. Buckingham: Centre for Education and Employment Research, University of Buckingham.

Wilshaw, M (2014) North of England Education Conference 2014 – HCMI Speech, *Ofsted*, 15 January 2014. [online] Available at: www.ofsted.gov.uk/resources/north-of-england-education-conference-2014-hmci-speech (accessed 28 August 2014).

Pathways into secondary teaching

Paul Dickinson

INTRODUCTION

This chapter provides an outline of the main pathways into secondary teaching in England. It will give you an understanding of the key differences between these pathways so you can make an informed choice about which one best suits your experience, needs and personal circumstances. In England there are some subject areas, such as physical education, English and history, where recruitment is strong and entry onto these pathways is highly competitive, whereas application levels are lower and entry is thus easier in other subject areas, such as mathematics, computer science and physics. Where recruitment has been a challenge you will note that a range of schemes have been put in place to try and improve recruitment. These include bursaries and subject knowledge enhancement courses.

If you are interested in finding out about pathways to teaching in other countries in the UK the following websites are helpful:

○ Teach in Scotland: www.teachinscotland.org

○ Teacher Training and Education in Wales: http://teachertrainingcymru.org/home

○ Teacher Qualifications and Registration in Northern Ireland: www.deni.gov.uk/index/school-staff/teachers-teachinginnorthernireland_pg.htm

CONTEXT

England boasts a significant range of diverse pathways into secondary teaching. Most of these lead to the award of QTS although academies and free schools (as a result of government legislation in 2012) hold the freedom to appoint teachers who do not hold QTS and have not followed a training programme (Coughlan, 2014). This also applies to independent schools.

The different pathways into teaching in England are subject to change based on the priorities of different governments and politicians. In 2010 the DfE published a White Paper, *The Importance of Teaching*, which outlined the government's commitment to *'reform initial teacher training to increase the proportion of time trainees spend in the classroom'* (DfE, 2010, p 9). Following this policy paper England is now the only country in the UK where some pathways to gaining QTS do not need to involve a university. More recently, the DfE's response to the *Carter Review of Initial Teacher Training* (2015) suggests support for a move to more evidence-based teaching and an emphasis on improving the quality of mentoring for student teachers. This response is likely to shape training pathways in the near future.

This chapter focuses on the main routes that will offer you QTS, as 96 per cent of teachers in state-funded secondary schools hold the award (DfE, 2012). Currently these are:

o   undergraduate degrees with QTS;

o   university-led one-year postgraduate certificate of education courses (PGCE);

o   two-year Teach First programmes targeting 'high flying' graduates who commit to working in challenging schools;

o   School-Centred Initial Teacher Training (SCITT) programmes, which offer various options including PGCE validated by a university, School Direct (salaried and tuition) and QTS only;

o   School Direct, which may or may not involve universities and thus offers QTS only or PGCE.

Reflective task

As you read this chapter consider these questions.

o   Do you want to spend almost all your training in one school?

o   Do you want to gain some Masters credits as you train?

o   What subject knowledge support will you need?

o   What support will you need in terms of *how* to teach your specialist subject (known as 'subject pedagogy')?

MAIN PATHWAYS INTO SECONDARY TEACHING

Broadly, ITE pathways fall into two categories:

1.   undergraduate three- and four-year pathways, which are all university-led;

2.   shorter postgraduate pathways, which are either university-led or school-led.

It can be argued that '*All routes have outstanding provision within them*' (House of Commons Education Committee, 2012, p 9) and that there is '*... little doubt that partnership between schools and universities is likely to provide the highest-quality initial teacher education*' (ibid). This is a view supported by recent Ofsted reports, *The Good Teacher Training Guide* (Smithers and Robinson, 2013) and the *Carter Review of Initial Teacher Training*, which stated:

... sometimes universities will take the lead, sometimes and increasingly, it will be the schools that lead the way. However, neither can do it alone and our review has made recommendations that emphasise the strength of working together ...

(Carter, 2015, p 3)

Reflective task

○   What do you think are the main benefits of strong university involvement in the training process and what do you consider to be the main benefits of strong school involvement in the training process?

Common characteristics of all pathways leading to Qualified Teacher Status

All pathways in England that lead to QTS share some common criteria, including:

○   on entry a pass of at least a 'C' in mathematics and English at GCSE or equivalent;

○   a pass in the Skills Tests in literacy and numeracy;

○   being selected by a process that involves schools;

○   for postgraduate entry, the possession of a first degree from a UK university or equivalent and generally, but not exclusively, in the subject area you plan to teach;

○   a minimum of 120 days in at least two different school settings.

The proportion of time spent in each school setting can vary significantly depending upon the particular route and ITE provider. These settings provide you with practical classroom experience and opportunities to undertake academic study to give you the knowledge and understanding to teach successfully. You will be assessed on your teaching skills and currently this assessment will be against eight key Teachers' Standards together with standards of Professional and Personal Conduct (see Appendix).

Most accredited providers organise their training programmes around subject knowledge / subject pedagogy and professional or educational studies, the latter covering general pedagogical aspects and other matters that range from working with pupils for whom English is an additional language and special educational needs to behaviour management and safeguarding of pupils.

As part of the quality assurance process all accredited providers of QTS receive regular inspections from Ofsted. It would be worth looking at the Ofsted report for your preferred providers at www.gov.uk/government/organisations/ofsted but be aware that this is only one indicator available to help inform your decision about the quality of the provider.

UNDERGRADUATE PATHWAYS

There are only a few providers that offer undergraduate pathways into secondary teaching. These are often the largest teacher education universities nationally and they tend to offer either three-year or four-year courses that lead to a degree in the subject area (Bachelor of Arts, Bachelor of Science or Bachelor of Education) and the award of QTS. They are university-led and are often but not exclusively in shortage subject areas such as mathematics and the sciences. For example, Sheffield Hallam University provides three-year degrees with QTS in mathematics, sciences and design and technology while the University of Brighton offers an undergraduate degree in physical education with QTS. Some of these routes will accept access to the second year if you already have a foundation degree, HND (Higher National Diploma) or HNC (Higher National Certificate) or have completed at least a year of a degree course.

What does training on an undergraduate pathway involve?

Each university will structure its courses differently, but all these courses will provide the specialist knowledge to gain a named degree in the subject and the requisite training and support to enable you to qualify as a teacher. University modules are led by well-qualified experts in the field and the university will also use its established close partnership networks with schools to organise training in the school context. Usually there is more emphasis in the first year on academic study and developing subject knowledge linked to gaining some experience of teaching in schools. However, the second and final year(s) will almost certainly include a greater weighting towards school-based training.

A typical course will provide you with strong support, with an academic tutor allocated to oversee your progress at the university and a subject mentor in the school. The school-based subject mentor will normally have undertaken a mentor training programme that is quality assured by the university. On your school-based training you will receive visits from a representative from the university to observe your teaching (often as part of a joint observation with your school-based subject mentor). The visit will also ensure that you are making progress against agreed targets. You will be made aware throughout your training of your progress towards both the degree classification and meeting the required standards for QTS. Gradually the amount of time that you lead lessons and the number of lessons that you teach will increase. These will be in Key Stage 3 (usually 11–14 year-olds) and Key Stage 4 (usually 14–16 year-olds) and possibly Key Stage 5 (usually 16–18 year-olds).

Why choose an undergraduate pathway?

These courses appeal to candidates who are sure that teaching is the career for them. They often attract applicants from a young age, some straight from sixth form. In most cases you will be making a commitment of at least three years before you embark on your career, although you could decide during the course that you only wish to pursue the degree. This is not recommended as so much of the emphasis of these courses is on preparing you to be an effective teacher in your subject. These courses do have the distinct advantage of spreading the school-based experience across three years and making the subject knowledge teaching particularly relevant to the classroom context. The more extended nature of the courses also enables greater opportunities for school-based research and more established relationships with schools. It means that you could be qualified and hold a degree in only three years whereas the majority of applicants for teacher training courses need to complete a first degree and then a one-year postgraduate course.

Students choosing an undergraduate course were very clear about why they had opted for what is effectively a degree with integrated teacher training. Students on the same three-year BSc Science with Education and QTS programme shared a range of reasons for their choices.

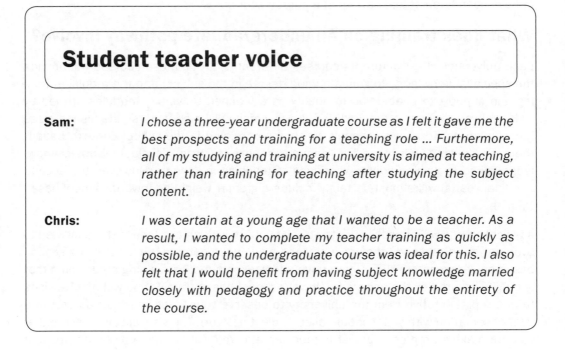

Student teacher voice

Sam: *I chose a three-year undergraduate course as I felt it gave me the best prospects and training for a teaching role … Furthermore, all of my studying and training at university is aimed at teaching, rather than training for teaching after studying the subject content.*

Chris: *I was certain at a young age that I wanted to be a teacher. As a result, I wanted to complete my teacher training as quickly as possible, and the undergraduate course was ideal for this. I also felt that I would benefit from having subject knowledge married closely with pedagogy and practice throughout the entirety of the course.*

POSTGRADUATE PATHWAYS

These pathways build upon subject knowledge already demonstrated through A levels or equivalent qualifications and, more importantly, a first degree. Due to the emphasis on developing pedagogy in what is normally a nine-month course, there is an expectation that you will bring significant subject knowledge of your field to the training, usually from a subject-specific degree.

However, for some subjects where there is a shortage of teachers, for example, in mathematics, physics, chemistry, computing, design and technology, or languages, there are courses available to both 'top up' your subject knowledge and fill some of the subject knowledge 'gaps' before qualifying to teach. These are government-funded Subject Knowledge Enhancement (SKE) courses (see Chapter 6).

The accredited provider that you select will identify if you need to complete an SKE course as part of the selection process and you might be offered a teacher training place on the condition that you undertake and successfully complete an SKE course. It could even be the case that you have relevant professional experience, and an SKE course will show you how to apply that to the curriculum and your teaching.

These SKE courses may be particularly useful if you are an overseas applicant where your degree is relevant, but where important content and curriculum knowledge have not been covered. You will not have to pay for an SKE course and at the time of writing, you may also be able to access an SKE bursary.

For some of the hard-to-recruit subjects there are scholarships and bursaries available to attract applicants and which reward high degree classifications. Refer to www.education.gov.uk/get-into-teaching/funding/postgraduate-funding for more details.

Reflective task

In order to start identifying your subject knowledge strengths and subject knowledge gaps, undertake the following exercise.

o List your degree modules, A levels (or equivalent) and GCSEs (or equivalent) relevant to your subject choice.

o Describe your subject knowledge development gained through personal experience – eg for PE playing for a club, for RE belonging to a particular faith.

o List the subject knowledge gained from your own reading, watching television or DVDs etc.

o Note down your understanding of effective ways of teaching the subject from observing lessons in schools.

o Now compare your knowledge with what is required to teach Key Stages 3 and 4 in your subject area (national curriculum docments are a good place to start for Key Stage 3 and current GCSE syllabuses are a good place to start for Key Stage 4).

Postgraduate pathways: university-led

This is the most established pathway into secondary teaching and involves a university awarding the postgraduate certificate, working in close partnership with schools which are quality assured by the university. The externality of the university quality assuring this process is one of the key benefits of this pathway. You will follow a programme that has been designed by the university and its partnership schools, which is likely to last approximately nine months. Even though this is university-led, approximately two-thirds of your time will be spent on school-based training so there is a strong emphasis on gaining classroom expertise in the relevant key stages, supported by teachers in the schools. The balance between experience gained in the school context and university-based sessions provides an excellent structure to enact Kolb's (1984) theory of experiential learning.

Kinchin (2011, p 33) summarises Kolb's experiential learning cycle as *'a continuous cyclical process of experience, reflection, theory and preparation – [where] the ability to learn can commence at any point in the cycle'*. As Kinchin continues, the individual elements of the sequence consist of:

○ *Experience: represents an active experience where new information is fed in.*

○ *Reflection: process of learning change, the individual now passively thinks about what has just happened.*

○ *Theory: the individual thinks about the new information and now contrasts this with other ideas and theories.*

○ *Preparation: this is where the learner considers what to do next.*

(Kinchin, 2011, p 33)

At the university you will experience taught sessions that cover subject knowledge and subject pedagogy (eg approaches to teaching Shakespeare in English) and professional or educational studies sessions that address the broader requirements of effective teaching in the school context (eg differentiation, meeting pupils' individual needs). Masters-level assignments support your professional learning and development and reinforce classroom-based activities. Credits gained within the postgraduate certificate programme can often be offset against a full Masters degree, depending upon the university where you complete your Masters degree. This will need investigating; do not assume that another university will allow you 40, 60 or indeed 120 credits from your PGCE course to be accredited against a Masters degree in their university. The university will support you in meeting the requirements for writing at Masters level and the required level of critical thinking and reflection.

For these pathways the university decides which schools to work in partnership with to facilitate the training programme. The university will then allocate you to the schools it considers will best meet both your needs and the overall training requirements. Thus, the university would consider issues associated with distance and childcare responsibilities, for example, and would use its knowledge of its partnership schools to try to select contrasting experiences (eg inner city / rural, advantaged catchment / disadvantaged catchment, 11–16 / 11–18 age range).

What does the training on a university-led postgraduate pathway involve?

University-led options enable you to work in an academic environment closely supported by a university tutor and to work closely with other students in your subject area. This peer network can provide a highly positive and supportive study and work environment. You are likely to have excellent library resources available and a virtual learning environment from the university, as well as expert lecturers who are aware of and are sometimes conducting the latest research relating to their specialism.

Who is this for?

University-led pathways suit applicants wanting Masters-level credits and links to further study in their early professional development. It is also likely that the university will be able to select from a large range of schools which ones will best suit your development. In many cases these pathways provide a more gradual immersion into the school environment with time to reflect on early learning away from the school context.

Student teacher voice

Sarah explains her reasoning for choosing a university-led course:

> *It combines both the mentoring and research support from the university and the wide range of practical teaching experience. [It] provides a lot of support and induction for students before their placements, which allows them to have an idea of best practice instead of jumping straight into the classroom.*

She comments that such courses:

> *also provide the opportunity to get credits towards a Masters qualification. This increases your job prospects but also allows you to take an active role in the education community.*

Sarah's comment shows the lack of clarity about different pathways to QTS among ITE applicants and student teachers, as a PGCE can also be taken through school-led courses, but perhaps also illustrates how much the PGCE is valued.

Another student teacher, **Jamie**, noted:

> *the support and specialist knowledge and experience provided by the university's staff is invaluable but there can sometimes be a sense of 'disconnect' between the university and school.*

Postgraduate pathways: School Direct

School Direct now accounts for approximately half of all national postgraduate numbers and this proportion is likely to increase. There are two main pathways available in School Direct; one is a salaried option, the other a tuition fee option.

Pathway 1: School Direct (salaried)

This pathway to QTS is aimed mainly at graduates with three or more years' relevant experience. You might have been a teaching assistant or you may have worked in another related context. However, schools can decide to accept applications from pro- spective students with less than three years' work experience to attract high quality can- didates in hard-to-fill subjects (eg mathematics and physics). You would be employed as an unqualified teacher on this pathway. NCTL provides funding to lead schools to cover training costs and subsidise student teacher salaries. This pathway carries the award of QTS and some programmes may also lead to an award at postgraduate level which includes Masters credits if the training is in partnership with a university.

○   **What does training on a School Direct pathway 1 (salaried) involve?** On this pathway you spend most of your time in the school where you are employed and you will gradually build up your contact time with classes and be supported by a school-based mentor who will advise, observe you teach and guide you through the process to meet the training requirements.

○   **Who is it for?** This pathway would suit those keen to work in a particular school and who have gained confidence in education-related work prior to beginning this pathway. As you will be a member of the school staff you will tend to be treated with the expectations commensurate of an established member of staff.

Pathway 2: School Direct (tuition fee)

In this pathway you will be selected by a lead school / schools, with the school or cluster of schools 'intending to employ you' at the end of your training. This does not mean that you have to take employment with them at the end of your training period but you may well have that option. You are likely to be based mostly in one host school and be sup- ported by a mentor and class teachers. You will be deeply immersed in the host school from very early on in your training and you will have regular access to practitioners in your field. It should also be noted that some School Direct courses involve working very closely with a university and enable you to gain a PGCE as well as QTS. This might mean some attendance at the university and undertaking some distance learning, particularly to support the academic aspects of your work.

○   **What does training on a School Direct pathway 2 (tuition fee) postgraduate course involve?** On this pathway you will spend most of your time in school, but will be provided with training agreed by the accredited provider which will cover areas like lesson planning, assessment, effective teaching and learning, as well as training in subject pedagogy. These inputs could be from specialists within the cluster of schools, but might also involve experts from outside the cluster, including from a university. There may be some travel to the local provider or the provider may organise for external experts to run sessions in the school, and sometimes distance learning materials will be used. If the final award is a PGCE then there will be training in writing and reflecting at Masters level.

○   **Who is it for?** This pathway would suit applicants keen to join a course that is strongly school-led and where you are keen to know which schools are being used for your training within the cluster. The level of school input will vary significantly depending upon the model agreed with the accredited provider. It is worth checking the intended structure for the year as the number of schools being used and the role of the accredited provider can vary significantly.

Reflective task

○ Consider what experience of education you can bring to your training programme and what detailed knowledge you have of the school context to help you decide whether a salaried pathway is appropriate.

Student teacher voice

Jeff explains why he chose this route:

The school where I was working decided to offer places in my subject. I thought it would give me a better chance of getting a 'foot in the door' and better employment opportunities. Places on other university-based ITE courses were being reduced drastically, and as a former student at the university accrediting the training I thought I would have a better chance of being accepted.

Joe felt that the school-led approach supported by the university was a strength:

The most positive aspects have been the quality of training we have received from our university tutor; I feel it has been of a very high standard. I also believe that it has been a great help to have had more time to get to know my mentor and the humanities department at my school than I may otherwise have done on a different course.

Peter comments: *I wanted to be in the classroom from day one ...*

Laura reflected: *To fully immerse myself within education was the way forward for me ...*

Research focus

British Education Research Association (BERA) (2014) *The Role of Research in Teacher Education: Reviewing the Evidence. Interim Report*.

The debate regarding the value and purpose of research in relation to teacher education is ongoing. This publication explores different teaching systems in the UK and internationally and argues that there is an important relationship between research and ongoing improvement in teacher education.

OTHER PATHWAYS TO QUALIFIED TEACHER STATUS

In a commitment to attract as broad a range of recruits into teaching as possible, there are now many different pathways offering routes to QTS. Some of these routes have been designed to attract and support secondary teaching applicants who might not otherwise have considered the profession, while others offer alternative routes to those explored above to attract a wider range of potential applicants. Some of the main pathways are summarised below.

Teach First

Teach First is an educational charity committed to working in partnership with schools to ensure that no child's educational success is limited by their socio-economic background. Its mission is driven by five key goals to be achieved by 2022 (Teach First, 2012). These goals aim to:

1. narrow the gap in literacy and numeracy at primary school (the aim is to narrow the gap by 90 per cent between pupils from low income communities and those from more affluent backgrounds);

2. narrow the gap in GCSE attainment at secondary school (between those gaining five GCSEs A*–C and those gaining eight GCSEs A*–C);

3. ensure young people develop key strengths, including resilience and well-being, to support high aspirations;

4. narrow the gap in the proportion of young people who are and are not in education, employment or training one year after compulsory education;

5. narrow the gap in university graduation, including from the top 25 per cent most selective universities (this refers to the gap between those from low socio-economic backgrounds and those from more affluent backgrounds).

Teach First also works extremely closely with a small number of selected universities as the accredited providers offering the PGCE award. The Masters-level credits gained for the PGCE can be built upon to gain a Masters degree in the field of education and leadership. Teach First is the second top graduate destination according to *The Times Top 100 Graduate Employers* in 2014, ahead of both Deloitte and the NHS (Milkround, 2015).

What does training with Teach First involve?

Teach First is a two-year pathway into teaching and is employment-based. You will be paid as a non-qualified teacher during the two-year training period. Some Teach First students do leave after two years, but many stay on much longer in the profession or continue in an educational role, often with Teach First.

This pathway includes a summer school of six weeks prior to the course commencement which focuses upon developing your subject knowledge and subject pedagogy and provides some school experience. You will then be allocated one school where almost all your teaching and training will take place and you will have a short second school placement. The selection of the schools for the Teach First route is determined by a points system which takes into consideration not only economic deprivation among pupils but also the local achievement gap between poorer children and their wealthier peers. The criteria mean that 36 per cent of English secondary schools are eligible to work with Teach First.

Despite the sometimes challenging nature of the schools that you will be employed in, retention rates for student teachers are good and there is significant wrap-around support from the employing school with a professional mentor and subject mentor, and university tutors who make regular visits to see student teachers in school. You will also be supported by a Teach First Leadership Development Officer (LDO) who is usually someone who has recently completed the Teach First pathway into teaching. Teach First recruited approximately 1000 secondary student teachers in 2014 (Teach First, 2014) out of a national total of 12,943 secondary student teachers (DfE, 2014b).

Who is it for?

This pathway is particularly relevant for highly qualified graduates who believe they can make a positive impact in some of the most challenging schools in England. There is a strong leadership dimension to the training, which is emphasised during your second year once you have gained your PGCE. This pathway would thus be good for those ambitious to take on an educational leadership role early in their career.

Information regarding Teach First applications can be found at https://apply.teachfirst.org.uk/

Student teacher voice

Some of the reasons applicants chose Teach First are presented below. **Jasmine** provides a rationale for her choice:

> *... after further research into the Teach First graduate scheme, I quickly became captivated with their life-changing movement that 'no child's educational success should be limited by their socio-economic background'. I felt a strong determination to become part of this movement for social change and to address educational disadvantage ... Not to mention, I wanted to rise to the challenge of teaching in a more disadvantaged area with a high level of responsibility in a school from day one.*

While **Simon** reflects that:

> *For me, getting straight into the classroom was crucial. Teach First offered that rapid advance into the profession. Teach First is aspirational in its aims*

and instils in you that you can make a difference to children's lives; the Teach First philosophy was crucial to me entering the profession via the charity.

Some of the positive features of the course are captured by **Jasmine**:

There is no doubt that the incredible level of support a Teach First participant receives is a key positive feature about this pathway into teaching, from university tutors, to in-school mentors, to continual CPD and subject development days ... Personally, I love the fact that Teach First is a two-year programme, with the PGCE year and NQT year both being completed in a full-time paid position in the same school.

She also recognises that this pathway provides significant challenges:

... you're in at the deep end with a much heavier timetable compared to other pathways into teaching, despite having less training prior to setting foot in the classroom.

Troops to Teachers

If you are ex-Service personnel, you can find out how the skills and experience gained in the Armed Forces can enable you to become an outstanding teacher. This scheme recognises prior expertise in the Services and non-graduates can gain places on this programme. More details can be found at www.education.gov.uk/get-into-teaching/troops-to-teachers.

Ex-Service leavers who hold a degree are also given extra support to enter teaching with, at present, an additional incentive of a bursary 'uplift' payment of £20,000 (DfE, 2015b).

Assessment Only

This pathway is for those of you who are experienced as teachers, who hold a degree and have been employed without having QTS. This pathway is not a training pathway but one where you will be assessed against the standards for QTS in your current employment. This process usually takes approximately three months. You would need to apply to an accredited provider that offers the Assessment Only pathway and be accepted onto the pathway. There will then be a period where you need to provide the necessary evidence against the standards for QTS and be assessed against these by a representative from the accredited provider. For more information see:

www.education.gov.uk/get-into-teaching/teacher-training-options/assessment-only

School-Centred Initial Teacher Training (SCITT)

Those consortia of schools that have been given government approval as accredited providers to run their own training are called SCITTs and '*provide practical, hands-on teacher training delivered by experienced, practising teachers based in their own school or at a school in their network'* (NCTL, nd).

SCITTs generally offer a range of pathways for student teachers to gain QTS, including the pathways mentioned above (PGCE, School Direct Salaried, School Direct Tuition and Assessment Only). SCITTs operate as providers of ITE in the same ways as universities, rather than offering alternative pathways into teaching. SCITTs which offer a PGCE course with QTS have programmes that are validated in partnership with a university. The university 'quality assures' the academic strand of the PGCE while the schools in the SCITT consortium 'quality assure' the school-based aspects of gaining QTS.

SCITTs benefit from being a cluster of schools from which expertise to support training can be drawn. It is also likely that a SCITT can tailor the course very closely to meet individual needs.

If you have prior experience in school, either as an unqualified teacher or as a Teaching Assistant, a SCITT should offer excellent training. Claire, a SCITT manager noted that often SCITTs are the preferred option for applicants who *don't want to leave the school environment, and in their words, return to a university-style course'.*

CONCLUSION

The aim of this chapter has been to provide you with an outline of the main pathways into secondary teaching. It is vital that you explore your chosen route in some depth by contacting your preferred accredited provider, as the distinction between university-led and school-led training is becoming increasingly blurred. There are now training programmes wholly based in schools but where university tutors contribute significantly to the training in the school, and university-led routes which are very strongly shaped by their partnership schools; each provider of ITE offers a selection of pathways so your choice is wide and varied.

☑ Progress Checklist

Reflective tasks

As you have read this chapter you will have undertaken a range of reflective tasks to help you understand the various pathways into teaching in England. You should have considered:

○ the main differences between university-led and school-led ITE;

○ the need for significant subject knowledge before being accepted onto a course;

○ the differences between QTS only and a PGCE.

Next steps

It is now worth identifying your first choice pathway. Write a short rationale for your decision. This would provide an excellent summary for what is likely to be your first question at interview: 'Why have you applied for this course?'

Look at the UCAS profiles for a selection of pathways that you are interested in and register for some Open Days with universities and schools. It is worth noting that many universities working with School Direct partners, including SCITTs, will also invite representatives from these pathways to their Open Days and vice versa.

▶▶ **TAKING IT FURTHER**

Department for Education (DfE) (2011) *Training Our Next Generation of Outstanding Teachers: Implementation Plan.*

This outlined the Coalition Government's plans for shaping ITE, much of which has now been implemented.

Get into Teaching website: www.education.gov.uk/get-into-teaching/teacher-training-options

The excellent 'Get into Teaching' website is operated by the National College for Teaching and Leadership (NCTL) and provides advice to help you choose between different pathways, including case studies, testimonials and links to teaching events.

University of Bristol (2015) *Handbook for Education Professionals: The Bristol Guide 2015.* Bristol: Graduate School of Education.

Written for all education professionals, the first chapter presents a comprehensive overview of different pathways into teaching.

Blogs and twitter feeds

The following links give access to information about different pathways into teaching:

Get into Teaching YouTube channel (including video blogs from teachers who followed different pathways): www.youtube.com/user/getintoteaching/videos (accessed 7 October 2015).

National College of Teaching and Leadership: @the_college

REFERENCES

Carter (2015) *Carter Review of Initial Teacher Training (ITT)*. [online] Available at: www.gov.uk/government/publications/carter-review-of-initial-teacher-training (accessed 13 February 2015).

Coughlan, S (2014) Highest ever number of school staff, *BBC Education News*. [online] Available at: www.bbc.co.uk/news/education-26973916 (accessed 14 August 2015).

Department for Education (DfE) (2010) *The Importance of Teaching*. Norwich: The Stationery Office.

Department for Education (DfE) (2012) *Academies to Have Same Freedom as Free Schools over Teachers*. [online] Available at: www.gov.uk/government/news/academies-to-have-same-freedom-as-free-schools-over-teachers (accessed 29 July 2015).

Department for Education (DfE) (2013a) *Troops to Teachers* [online] Available at: www.education.gov.uk/get-into-teaching/troops-to-teachers (accessed 20 February 2015).

Department for Education (DfE) (2013b) *Assessment Only Route to QTS*. [online] Available at: www.education.gov.uk/get-into-teaching/teacher-training-options/assessment-only (accessed 20 February 2015).

Department for Education (DfE) (2014a) *Subject Knowledge Enhancement Courses*. [online] Available at: https://getintoteaching.education.gov.uk/subject-knowledge-enhancement-ske-courses (accessed 20 February 2015).

Department for Education (DfE) (2014b) *Initial Teacher Training Census for the Academic Year 2014 to 2015* [online]. Available at: www.gov.uk/government/uploads/system/uploads/attachment_data/file/380175/ITT_CENSUS_2014-15_FINAL.pdf (accessed 20 July 2015).

Department for Education (DfE) (2015a) *Get into Teaching: School Direct*. [online] Available at: https://getintoteaching.education.gov.uk/explore-my-options/school-led-training/school-direct (accessed 25 September 2015).

Department for Education (DfE) (2015b) *Get into Teaching: Troops to Teachers Postgraduate Route*. [online] Available at: https://getintoteaching.education.gov.uk/explore-my-options/secondary-training-options/troops-to-teachers-postgraduate-route (accessed 20 July 2015).

House of Commons Education Committee (2012) *Great Teachers: Attracting, Training and Retaining the Best (Ninth Report of the Session 2010–12)*. London: The Stationery Office Limited.

Kinchin, G D (2011) Understanding Learning, in Ellis, V (ed) *Learning and Teaching in Secondary Schools*. 4th ed. Exeter: Learning Matters.

Kirk, G (2013) *The Value of University and School Partnerships in Teacher Education*. London: Universities' Council for the Education of Teachers (UCET).

Kolb, D A (1984) *Experiential Learning: Experience as the Source of Learning and Development*. Vol. 1. Englewood Cliffs, NJ: Prentice-Hall.

Milkround (2015) *The Times Top 100 Graduate Employers.* [online] Available at: www. milkround.com/staticpages/12680/the-times-top-100-graduate-employers/ (accessed 20 February 2015).

National College for Teaching and Leadership (NCTL) (n.d.) National College for Teaching and Leadership homepage. [online] Available at: www.gov.uk/government/ organisations/national-college-for-teaching-and-leadership (accessed 20 February 2015).

Ofsted (2014) *Initial Teacher Education: Inspection Statistics Sept 2013 to Aug 2014.* [online] Available at: www.gov.uk/government/collections/initial-teacher-education-inspections-and-outcomes (accessed 20 February 2015).

Ofsted reports (n.d.) [online] Available at: https://www.gov.uk/topic/schools-colleges-childrens-services/inspections#survey-reports (accessed 3 December 2015).

Smithers, A and Robinson P (2013) *The Good Teacher Training Guide.* [online] Available at: www.buckingham.ac.uk/wp-content/uploads/2014/01/GTTG2013.pdf (accessed 13 February 2015).

Teach First (n.d.) Teach First homepage [online] Available at: www.teachfirst.org.uk/ (accessed 20 February 2015).

Teach First (2012) *Teach First Launches Five Steps to Reducing Inequality in Education.* [online] Available at: www.teachfirst.org.uk/press/teach-first-launches-five-steps-reducing-inequality-education (accessed 1 July 2015).

Teach First (2014) *Our Impact.* [online] Available at: www.teachfirst.org.uk/sites/default/ files/press/pdf/impact%20doc%20WEB.pdf (accessed 20 July 2015).

UCAS (n.d.) UCAS homepage. [online] Available at: www.ucas.com/ucas/teacher-training (accessed 20 February 2015).

Secondary teaching today

Mel Norman

INTRODUCTION

This chapter focuses on education policy and its impact on secondary teachers and their teaching. Education policy is decided by the government of the day, which means that politics and education are inextricably linked. This is a fact that you should be aware of if you are thinking of becoming a teacher. Policy changes to the curriculum, public examinations and teacher professionalism are all discussed in this chapter, as well as the significant influence of Ofsted and the impact of new technologies on teaching and learning in the secondary school.

The chapter also outlines the diverse nature of schools and offers you an opportunity to reflect on the challenges of working In a variety of school environments.

THE INFLUENCE OF GOVERNMENT POLICY

Government policy has an impact on virtually every aspect of secondary school structures, from the buildings, to teachers' contracts, to the curriculum and the examination system. Dillon and Maguire (2011) make an important point in regard to schools' and teachers' responsibilities in complying with government policy:

> schools and teachers have to be familiar with, and able to enact, policies that are planned for them by others and they are held accountable for this task.
>
> (Dillon and Maguire, 2011, p 29)

It is important that you are aware of the influences of government policy but this is not something that should put you off becoming a teacher as the whole process of training and being part of a school community will prepare you to manage change and be successful in your career.

At the time of writing this chapter we have been through a period of immense government influence on education, which has caused widespread concern among teachers. Governments change and policies change with governments, thus the influence of government policy on education is an ongoing process. Even if a policy directive eventually proves to be unworkable, schools and the teaching workforce will have had to implement the policy before it is deemed unworkable and this is something you need to be prepared for in teaching.

The biggest impact on education since the 1944 Education Act, which embraced universal and free secondary education for all children, came with the 1988 Education Reform

Act (ERA) which gave the Secretary of State for Education 451 new powers (Adams, 2014). The ERA was implemented during a Conservative government term of office but had its origins in the 1976 'Ruskin speech' given by James Callaghan, the then Labour Prime Minister, which generated the Great Debate about education that took place over a number of years (ASCL, 2013). When the Labour Party came to power again in 1997, Tony Blair's three priorities for government in his pre-election speech were '*education, education, education*'.

The major political parties have had a great influence on education policy during the past 35 years. However, some policy changes cause more unrest among teachers than others. The disenchantment generated among the teaching profession by 'Govian reforms' is thought to have resulted in that particular Secretary of State for Education, Michael Gove, being removed from office in July 2014 in an effort to regain the support of teachers prior to the General Election of May 2015. Some of the policies introduced during the Govian era have supposedly given many schools increased freedom and the autonomy to make decisions which are not influenced by government but are influenced by the local needs of the individual school and the community which that school serves. Whether this is in fact the case is dependent on the circumstances of each individual school, but ultimately the Secretary of State for Education has the final say. One result of government policy is that there is now a complex structure of secondary schools so although you may have spent approximately 13 years of your life in the English school system, there will be significant differences from your own experiences of school.

Reflective task

o   Do you agree with politicians having so much influence on the education system? What are the pros and cons of them doing so?

o   How well do you think you will be able to cope with changes imposed on the education system by successive governments of varying political persuasion?

Research focus

Adams, P (2014) *Policy and Education*. Abingdon: Routledge.

In this book, Paul Adams traces the influence of government policy on education over the last 30 years. He identifies two key trends.

1.   Political opinion has significantly shaped educational policy in that time.

2.   There has been an increasing concern that education policy should seek to measure the 'performance' of pupils, teachers and schools. This has led to a growth in the number of educational 'performance indicators' used that do not always have a positive impact on what takes place in schools.

TYPES OF SECONDARY SCHOOL

Since 2010 the Coalition government set about reforms to school organisation with the aim of enabling a wider range of providers of schooling to address the specific needs of local communities and parents. One of the biggest changes since 2010 is the increased number of schools which are now academies.

Academies

Academies were first established by the Labour government in 2000 with the aim of driving up standards in schools that were deemed to be under-performing or failing in relation to Ofsted inspection criteria. Although state-maintained, this first tranche of academies were independent schools which accrued further support (not necessarily direct funding) from various sponsors in an effort to improve standards. Sponsors included individual people, local companies and church foundations. The Coalition government of 2010 expanded the academies programme, enabling a wider range of schools to become academies should they wish. In January 2010, there were 199 secondary academies open and operating; by December 2014 there were 1702 secondary academies open and operating (DfE, 2015a).

- ○ Academies are run by a trust which employs the academy staff and although state funded, the money comes directly from central government not from the local authority (LA).

- ○ Academy sponsors include businesses, academy chains and universities.

- ○ Academy sponsors have a responsibility for improving performance in the academies they sponsor.

In addition, academies:

- ○ do not have to follow the national curriculum;

- ○ are allowed to set their own length of school day;

- ○ decide their own term dates and are allowed to operate outside the limits of national pay and conditions for teaching staff;

- ○ are subject to inspections by Ofsted;

- ○ must adhere to national guidelines in regard to admissions, special educational needs and exclusions.

Traditional academies are those which were established before 2010 when only failing or under-performing schools could be awarded academy status.

Converter academies are generally existing, high-achieving schools which have opted out of LA control as a result of the Coalition government's policy of widening access to academy status.

Teacher voice

Liz's view: what is it like working in an academy?

We became an academy quite early on after the Conservative-Liberal Democrat coalition was accelerating the idea for those schools that were performing well at the time. The positives of being an academy include slightly improved finance and it allowed the school more autonomy over what is done with land and buildings, helping us to achieve our own priorities. For example, we were able to develop an old building into a Sixth Form Centre and reopen the Sixth Form, after the LA closed it a few years ago. We still follow national pay and conditions for teachers so that is not of concern at present. We also have more autonomy with setting our own term dates but this can annoy a few parents because the holiday dates might not always fit in with local primary schools.

It would be helpful if you could make your own enquiries about the success, or otherwise, of academies in your own home area; it would be even better if you can talk to teachers working in academies to get their perspectives.

Free schools

Free schools come under the umbrella of academies but they are new schools which have been given permission to develop after a group of like-minded people, eg parents, teachers, universities or employers, have submitted proposals to the DfE which have been accepted.

Teacher voice

Paul's view: what is it like working in a free school?

Free schools are bound to their 'funding agreement' proposal as they are directly funded by the DfE and strictly audited by the DfE. Any detail about a free school, therefore, is entirely specific to that one school. Many free schools, including mine, are in temporary sites in buildings which were not originally schools.

Generally:

○ *class sizes are smaller than the national average (our maximum class size is 25);*

○ *staffing is younger than in an LA school;*

○ *we try to offer staff higher pay than they would expect working in the maintained sector;*

○ *we teach slightly over the allocation of other secondary schools, but this time also includes supervising 'prep' and running enrichment activities;*

○ *we are allowed to employ unqualified teachers if the person is right for the job;*

○ *we have the freedom to design our own curriculum and assessment system;*

○ *we start early (doors open at 8am) and finish late with an extended day (4.20pm or 5.30pm for clubs).*

City Technology Colleges

City Technology Colleges (CTCs) were established in urban areas in the early 1990s as an outcome of the ERA, focusing on technology subjects, including mathematics and science, and working in close liaison with local businesses. The majority of the 15 CTCs have subsequently converted to academies but a new type of school, University Technical Colleges (UTCs) (see below), has developed to bridge the technology gap.

University Technical Colleges

UTCs are established in particular areas to offer 14–18 year-olds a curriculum which focuses on technical and scientific subjects. They work in partnership with university departments and local employers to develop scientists, engineers and technicians for future types of employment, many of which are as yet unknown. UTCs are government funded but are outside the remit of the LA so are part of the suite of schools under the umbrella term 'academy'.

Maintained schools

Maintained schools are funded through LAs. LAs have had less and less to do with schools in their local area as schools change into academies. Maintained schools must follow the national curriculum and must adhere to national pay and conditions regarding the employment of teachers. There are four types of maintained schools, each of which is briefly discussed below.

Community schools

These are entirely in the control of the LA, which is responsible for employing the staff as well as setting the admissions policy and owning and maintaining the buildings and land.

Teacher voice

Mark's view: what is it like to work in a community school?

The positive of working in a community school used to be the additional support from the LA providing, for example, educational psychologists and Traveller Support but this has changed and most of these services are now bought in. When there are issues with building work the LA is liable so money can be made available. We have clear contracts which have sensible hours and we also have more security; if academies fold, staff are left in limbo re contracts and pensions.

The negative is that we are tied to the national curriculum despite feeder primaries that are academies not having to teach it. We are restricted on what we can pay staff, so in theory in shortage subjects academies may find it easier to recruit.

Grammar schools

In some parts of the country, LAs have kept the 11+ examination so selective grammar schools are still in existence.

Teacher voice

Kate's view: what is it like to work in a selective grammar school?

The positives of working in a selective school are that academic achievement is not frowned upon by other pupils. Pupils don't tend to mock each other for their academic achievement. There is also a competitive edge to achievement in and out of the classroom. Most students have worked hard to be at the school and this is evident in their attitude towards studying; they want to do well and want to know how to improve. In the comprehensive schools that I have worked in, students were more reluctant to put their hands up or get involved in a class discussion. This is not the case in our school; the students always want to be involved and have their say.

However, there can be an undercurrent of entitlement, by that I mean they automatically expect to get good grades. On the other hand, students can become overwhelmed with what is expected of them and this means some become disengaged as they feel that they can't keep up with the rest of their peer group.

Kate's experience and perceptions show there are positives and negatives to working in a selective school, but of course there are positives and negatives to most workplaces.

Foundation schools

Although maintained by the LA, these are run by the governing body, which employs the teaching staff and sets the admissions criteria. The land and buildings may be owned by a charity.

Voluntary controlled schools

Voluntary controlled schools are run by the LA, which employs the teaching staff and sets the admissions policy. However, the land and buildings are very often owned by a charity, often a religious organisation.

Voluntary aided schools

Voluntary aided schools are usually faith schools and the religious organisation is likely to own the land and buildings. The governing body employs the teaching staff and decides the school's admissions policy.

Teacher voice

Graham's view: what is it like to work in a voluntary aided faith school?

The school is answerable to the Diocese, which can be constricting. The school's governors are our employers on behalf of the Diocese; however, we are contracted to the LA in terms of pay. As a faith school we receive funding from donations, grants, governors' funds and Catholic parishes, as each parish priest should pay a levy to the school for the children who live in the boundaries of their parish. Some of this funding contributes towards the extra 15 per cent we do not receive through the DfE but we need to arrange additional fundraising activities. We have appointed a Marketing and Fundraising Officer and have a formal alumni group and programme through Facebook and Twitter.

Independent schools

Schools which lie outside government control and funding are known as independent schools and they charge fees for attendance at the school. Most are charitable trusts and are not businesses set up to make a profit. Although independent in most senses, these schools have to be registered with the government and are subject to inspections by ISIS, the Independent Schools Inspection Service, along similar lines to the DfE inspection service, Ofsted.

Teacher voice

Chris's view: what is it like to work in an independent school?

It's important to note that there is a huge variation in the type and quality of independent schools. Therefore, experiences can vary enormously from school to school, making any generalisations difficult; however:

○   *there are fewer pupils per teaching group than in other types of school;*

○   *you rarely encounter disaffected, negative pupils or parents;*

○   *parental influence and parental expectation is significant with an element of 'getting results because we are paying for it';*

○   *contracts and expectations of teachers in independent schools often include long hours on site and compulsory duties during evenings and weekends, compensated by shorter terms.*

Reflective task

o   All schools vary; personal choice is an important aspect when selecting the school you want to work in. Having read about the variety of secondary schools in England, do you have a preference for working in one type of school? What has influenced your choice?

o   Do you think that the current organisation of schools has led to greater choice or to greater fragmentation, division and inequality? Explain your answer.

TEACHERS' PAY AND CONDITIONS OF SERVICE

A new Pay and Conditions document came into force in September 2013. From September 2014 teachers' pay may be linked to the performance of the pupils taught. The document applies to teachers who are employed by an LA or by the governing body of a voluntary aided or foundation school. The changes are summarised below from the DfE document (2014).

o   The removal of pay progression linked to length of service and the introduction of pay progression linked to performance.

o   The option for schools to increase an individual teacher's pay at different rates based on their performance.

o   Giving schools more freedom to determine the starting salaries of teachers new to the school.

o   Removing any obligation on schools when recruiting to match a teacher's existing salary.

Having one's 'performance' assessed to determine a pay level is a new aspect of being a teacher; the DfE (2014) document suggests the following could be considered when determining pay:

o   impact on pupil progress;

o   impact on wider outcomes for pupils;

o   improvements in specific elements of practice, such as behaviour management or lesson planning;

o   impact of effectiveness on teachers or other staff;

o   wider contribution to the work of the school.

Reflective task

o   What is your opinion on performance-related pay?

o   How do you think you might demonstrate evidence of effective performance, improvements in your practice, and the kinds of impact of the aspects referred to above?

If you do decide to become a teacher, you will be subject to the new pay and conditions which differ significantly from previous conditions of service, and which have caused a great deal of concern among many teachers. Since the DfE documentation suggests that pay rises linked to performance should draw on a range of evidence, the keeping of evidence is crucial throughout your professional life. You will begin to keep evidence about your teaching and the impact you have on pupil learning from the moment you start your training course. You will have to keep evidence of your achievement towards the Teachers' Standards (Appendix) throughout your training so that you may be recommended for the award of QTS at the end of your training. During your induction period when working as an NQT you will again need to keep evidence of achievement of the Teachers' Standards and you will have regular meetings and appraisals from appointed staff. At the end of your induction period, if you are successful QTS will be ratified and you will be a fully qualified teacher.

During your career you will continue to be subject to appraisal and be given feedback with specific reference to your planning, preparation and teaching, and the performance of the pupils you teach, specifically in terms of grades achieved in external exams. Your commitment to the wider community of the school, for example, running school clubs, or getting involved with the Duke of Edinburgh's Award Scheme, will also be monitored. Continuing to amass evidence of your achievement of the Teachers' Standards will enable you to apply for the upper pay range provided that the following criteria are met:

(a) *the teacher is highly competent in all elements of the relevant Standards; and*

(b) *the teacher's achievements and contribution to an educational setting or settings are substantial and sustained.*

(DfE, 2014, para 15.2)

Table 4.1 shows in detail the DfE 'Expectations of a teacher' which you would be wise to scrutinise as part of your thinking about whether secondary teaching is the right career for you.

Table 4.1 Expectations of a teacher (DfE, 2014, pp 44–45, para 52.1–52.16)

52.1 A teacher may be required to undertake the following duties:

Teaching

52.2 Plan and teach lessons to the classes they are assigned to teach within the context of the school's plans, curriculum and schemes of work.

52.3 Assess, monitor, record and report on the learning needs, progress and achievements of assigned pupils.

52.4 Participate in arrangements for preparing pupils for external examinations.

Whole school organisation, strategy and development

52.5 Contribute to the development, implementation and evaluation of the school's policies, practices and procedures in such a way as to support the school's values and vision.

52.6 Work with others on curriculum and/or pupil development to secure co-ordinated outcomes.

52.7 Supervise and so far as practicable teach any pupils where the person timetabled to take the class is not available to do so.

Health, safety and discipline

52.8 Promote the safety and well-being of pupils.

52.9 Maintain good order and discipline among pupils.

Management of staff and resources

52.10 Direct and supervise support staff assigned to them and, where appropriate, other teachers.

52.11 Contribute to the recruitment, selection, appointment and professional development of other teachers and support staff.

52.12 Deploy resources delegated to them.

Professional development

52.13 Participate in arrangements for the appraisal and review of their own performance and, where appropriate, that of other teachers and support staff.

52.14 Participate in arrangements for their own further training and professional development and, where appropriate, that of other teachers and support staff including induction.

Communication

52.15 Communicate with pupils, parents and carers.

Working with colleagues and other relevant professionals

52.16 Collaborate and work with colleagues and other relevant professionals within and beyond the school.

You should access the full document (see Reference list) for further details about working time and overarching rights (paras 52.17–53.10).

COLLEGE OF TEACHING

In December 2014 the DfE announced that a professional College of Teaching will be set up. The college is to be independent of government control, but there will be a government consultation on the setting up and running of the college. The aims of the college are to protect standards in education and to raise the status of the teaching profession in line with other professions such as medicine and law. The College of Teaching website makes the following claim:

> *The College of Teaching will be committed to the improvement of education through the support of teacher development and recognition of excellence in teaching. It will be led by teachers, enabling the teaching profession to take responsibility for its professional destiny, set its own aspirational standards and help teachers to challenge themselves to be ever better for those they serve.*

(www.collegeofteaching.com/)

Ofsted

All maintained schools and academies are subject to regular inspections by Ofsted. After an Ofsted inspection, a report is published which evaluates the effectiveness of a school. The main categories for inspection in secondary schools are:

○   qualities of leadership in and management of the school;

○   behaviour and safety of pupils;

○   quality of teaching in the school;

○   achievement of pupils at the school;

○   quality of education provided in the post-16 study programmes (where applicable).

Each category is awarded a grade by the Ofsted inspection team on a scale of 1–4:

1 = Outstanding

2 = Good

3 = Requires improvement

4 = Inadequate

If the overall evaluation report reflects grades 3 and 4, a school may be subject to specific intervention to bring about improvements or the school may be closed. As an early career teacher, you will have a significant part to play in an Ofsted inspection although be reassured that you will be given advice on preparation for the event by senior managers in the school. You can expect to be observed teaching by one of the Ofsted inspectors, and you may be interviewed about aspects of your teaching and about the school in general.

School management and appraisal systems include regular observations of teaching by senior members of staff undertaking 'learning walks'. These 'learning walks' enable senior managers to be fully aware of everything going on in the school.

> ## Reflective task
>
> ○ Do you think it is a positive move to have a College of Teaching with a similar remit to those who work in the medical professions (General Medical Council)?
>
> ○ Are you prepared to meet the expectations outlined in Table 4.1? Is there anything in the list of expectations that you would not be able to commit to?

CURRICULUM

The school curriculum encompasses everything which goes on within a school in terms of the experience of the pupils of that school. There are two strands to the school curriculum, the academic curriculum (subject teaching) and the pastoral curriculum (safeguarding and care of the pupils). Chapter 8 discusses the pastoral curriculum so this section will focus on the academic curriculum. All the core subjects (mathematics, English and science) are compulsory at Key Stages 1–4. Curriculum areas known as foundation subjects, ie art and design, design and technology, languages, geography, history, and music, are compulsory to the end of Key Stage 3. Other foundation subjects, citizenship, computing, PE and RE must be part of the curriculum at Key Stages 3 and 4.

The national curriculum

A national curriculum developed from the ERA in the 1980s; a suite of subjects was identified as statutory within the curricula of all state schools from Key Stages 1–4. There have been several revisions of the national curriculum since the late 1980s, the most recent one being in September 2014 (DfE, 2013a). However, with academies and independent schools being exempt from compliance with the national curriculum, it is hardly a 'national' curriculum. The original national curriculum documents comprised an A4 folder for each of the 12 subjects; every subsequent revision has been slimmer with the 2014 version being only three or four sides of A4 per subject. This less prescriptive approach with each revision should mean that the government has begun to trust the professionalism of teachers. However, in the context of performance-related pay and the general accountability that teachers and schools have to contend with, the professionalism of teachers still seems to be in question. Perhaps the newly established College of Teaching will be able to rekindle the former status of the teaching profession.

GCSE and A level examinations

At Key Stage 4 all pupils have to continue to study the core subjects of mathematics, English and science. Pupils must also be offered a course that enables them to study a subject from each of four subject areas:

o   the arts – comprising art and design, music, dance, drama and media arts;

o   design and technology;

o   the humanities – comprising history and geography;

o   modern foreign languages.

The Coalition government introduced changes to GCSEs and A levels, judging them to lack rigour, coupled with a concern about low literacy rates among school leavers (DfE, 2013b).

The major changes to GCSEs are:

o   grades will be awarded from 1–9 with 9 being the top grade;

o   assessment will mainly be by exam at the end of the course;

o   courses will be designed to be studied for two years;

o   fewer resit opportunities will be available.

The major changes to AS and A levels are:

o   assessment will mainly be by terminal exams;

o   AS assessment will take place after one year's study;

o   AS will be a 'stand-alone' qualification, no longer counting towards an A level;

o   A level assessment will take place after two years' study.

(DfE 2015b)

This major overhaul of the public examination system has caused a lot of controversy among the teaching workforce as never before have both GCSEs and A levels undergone reforms at the same time.

Research focus

Hirsch, E D (1998) *Cultural Literacy: What Every American Needs to Know.* New York: Vintage Books

E D Hirsch was a Yale University Professor of English Literature who advocated schools teaching what he calls 'cultural literacy', meaning the core knowledge of facts, concepts, phrases and literature that everyone needs in order to be a true citizen of the country in which they live. Michael Gove is an admirer of Hirsch's work and it had a key influence on the latest national curriculum, particularly in English and history.

Raising of the school leaving age

The Coalition government raised the school leaving age from 16 to 17 in 2013 and to 18 in 2015. Young people must now stay in some form of education or training until the age of 18. Options at the age of 16 are to remain at school or college; take up an apprenticeship or traineeship; or undertake part-time study supplemented with employment or voluntary work (DfE 2015c).

ASSESSMENT

Assessing learning and monitoring pupil progress underpin all of the Teachers' Standards and are explicit in TS2, TS4, TS5 and TS6 (see Appendix). Until 2013, teachers used level descriptors to assess pupils' learning and progression but level descriptors have not been published with the 2014 national curriculum. The DfE wants schools to introduce their own approaches to formative assessment to support pupil attainment and progression. Once again this has caused concern as there are no national benchmarks for tracking pupil progress at Key Stage 3. Many schools have retained the use of the levels they had previously been using, believing this to be a system understood by pupils, teachers and parents. Other schools have developed alternative systems but these seem similar to level descriptors but by another name, and some schools are working with the DfE to produce guidelines for assessment to be published in the future. Professional subject associations have worked on guidelines for assessment without levels, but being subject focused, they may not have general appeal in schools striving for a corporate approach to assessment policy.

Pupil achievement is a basic 'measure' of a school's overall performance and the annual publication of league tables can create tension in an increasingly competitive secondary school market. It is the DfE's belief that the changes to the school curriculum outlined in this section will create a more equitable approach to comparisons between institutions. The English Baccalaureate (EBacc) was introduced by the Coalition government in 2010. It is used to measure school performance by indicating how many pupils get grade C or above in what are classed as core academic subjects at Key Stage 4 in any government-funded school. The subjects are:

○   English;

○   mathematics;

○   history or geography;

○   the sciences;

○   a language.

In June 2015 the Conservative government announced that all pupils starting secondary school in September 2015 will take the EBacc subjects when they start their GCSEs in 2020 (DfE, 2015d).

Curriculum changes have been coupled with the development of the Pupil Premium where schools are allocated money to meet the needs of disadvantaged pupils in the school, the school being allowed to decide how that money is spent in order to best help pupils achieve their highest potential. A further measure, Progress 8, comes into effect in 2016/2017. The statistics will monitor pupil progress from the end of primary school to the end of secondary school as a 'value added' measure, comparing the achievements of pupils with others with the same prior attainment. It is believed this will be a fairer comparison than the current 'league table' system.

Progress 8 will measure:

○ attainment across eight subjects (mathematics and English + three highest point scores in science subjects, computer science, history, geography and languages + three highest point scores from any other subject not already included from the previous list, eg English literature, music, art);

○ progress across the same eight subjects;

○ percentage of pupils achieving grade C (or equivalent) in English and mathematics;

○ percentage of pupils achieving the English Baccalaureate (five subjects at a minimum of grade C (or equivalent) to include English and mathematics + a science subject, a humanities subject and a language).

These changes indicate the enormous responsibility that teachers have in regard to the assessment of pupils and progress in their learning. The currency of the Teachers' Standards coupled with the current accountability culture will keep you focused on the importance of assessment and will enable you to be successful in this aspect of your teaching career.

NEW TECHNOLOGIES

The pace of change in regard to technological support for teaching and learning is such that 'new' seems an inappropriate term. It is now rare for any classroom in a secondary school to be without access to the internet, a digital projector and an interactive whiteboard. Recently, the use of iPads has become the norm in the classroom, especially in academies and independent schools. Pupil work is stored electronically, marked and commented upon electronically and available electronically to all who need to access it, including the pupils themselves, teachers, form tutors, parents and carers. If you are coming into teaching from an environment where technology has not played a big part, you will need to become 'IT savvy' and be able to manipulate the technology creatively when planning and preparing for lessons.

Reflective task

○ Do you perceive government policy on the curriculum as 'interference', or does it reassure you that standards are being monitored with a drive for continuous improvement in schools, teaching and learning?

○ What are your thoughts on having a national curriculum if it is only statutory in a minority of secondary schools? Is there any point to it?

○ How would you use e-learning in your particular specialist subject to teach creative and engaging lessons?

CONCLUSION

The Conservative government, which took control in May 2015, is bound to make changes in the field of education, which will affect you in your decision about whether to seek to become a secondary school teacher. This chapter has outlined some of the policies imposed by governments that affect you at classroom level. The chapter has also given you an overview of the different types of secondary school that you may find yourself working in if and when you train to teach. You will thus have some idea of the differences between schools and will know what to look for that suits you personally if and when seeking a first post.

 Progress checklist

Reflective tasks

As you have read this chapter you will have undertaken tasks which asked you to reflect on the influence of government policy in education. You will have to decide whether you will be able to deal with this aspect of the teaching profession. This chapter has also outlined the range of schools available for you to teach in should you decide secondary teaching is for you.

Next steps

○ Look regularly at the education press and the DfE website to monitor changes that are affecting schools.

○ Research different types of school to see what type of school will best suit you personally if and when you search for and look to accept a first teaching post.

○ As suggested in Chapter 2, engage in visits to secondary schools but make sure you visit different types of school to see how they work in practice, and identify what differences there are between them.

▶▶ **TAKING IT FURTHER**

Hayes, D (ed) (2004) *Key Debates in Education*. Abingdon: RoutledgeFalmer.

40 chapters written by a range of authors covering various issues related to education encouraging discussion and debate.

Russi, J and Friel, R (2013) *How to Survive Working in a Catholic School*. Chawton: Redemptorist Publications.

Helpful advice if you are thinking of teaching in a Catholic school.

Ward, S and Eden, C (2009) *Key Issues in Education Policy*. London: Sage.

The authors examine government policy in relation to key areas, including the curriculum, academies and assessment.

Blogs and twitter feeds

It is really important to keep up to date with the latest developments in education. The following are useful starting points.

Rebecca Allen: http://rebeccaallen.co.uk/economics-of-education/ (accessed 1 October 2015)

Guardian Education news: @GuardianEdu

UK Education Matters: @SchoolDuggery

REFERENCES

Adams, P (2014) *Policy and Education*. Abingdon: Routledge.

Association of School and College Leaders (ASCL) (2013) *The Great Education Debate: Setting the Scene*. [online] Available at: www.greateducationdebate.org.uk/utilities/download.html?id=4C3EA1F9-807C-47DD-8F970FA93DD2524B (accessed 3 December 2015).

College of Teaching (n.d.) College of Teaching Homepage. [online] Available at: www.collegeofteaching.com/ (accessed 30 July 2015).

Department for Education (DfE) (2013a) *The National Curriculum in England*. [online] Available at: www.gov.uk/dfe/nationalcurriculum (accessed 30 July 2015).

Department for Education (DfE) (2013b) *Reforming Qualifications and the Curriculum to Better Prepare Pupils for Life after School*. [online] Available at: www.gov.uk/government/policies/reforming-qualifications-and-the-curriculum-to-better-prepare-pupils-for-life-after-school (accessed January 2015).

Department for Education (DfE) (2014) *School Teachers' Pay and Conditions Document 2013 and Guidance on School Teachers' Pay and Conditions*. [online] Available at: www.gov.uk/government/uploads/system/uploads/attachment_data/file/341951/School_teachers__pay_and_conditions_2014.pdf (accessed 2 May 2015).

Department for Education (DfE) (2015a) *Open Academies and Academy Projects Awaiting Approval: January 2015*. [online] Available at: www.gov.uk/government/publications/open-academies-and-academy-projects-in-development (accessed 30 July 2015).

Department for Education (DfE) (2015b) *Get the Facts: GCSE, AS and A Level Reform.* [online] Available at: www.gov.uk/government/publications/get-the-facts-gcse-and-a-level-reform (accessed 4 May 2015).

Department for Education (DfE) (2015c) *School Leaving Age.* [online] Available at: www.gov.uk/know-when-you-can-leave-school (accessed 4 May 2015).

Department for Education (DfE) (2015d) *English Baccalaureate (EBacc).* [online] Available at: www.gov.uk/government/publications/english-baccalaureate-ebacc/english-baccalaureate-ebacc (accessed 29 July 2015).

Dillon, J and Maguire, M (eds) (2011) *Becoming a Teacher: Issues in Secondary Education*. Maidenhead: Open University Press.

Hirsch, E D (1998) *Cultural Literacy: What Every American Needs to Know*. New York: Vintage Books.

University Technical Colleges (UTCS) (n.d.) University Technical Colleges homepage. [online] Available at: www.utcolleges.org (accessed 20 February 2015).

5 Professional learning as a secondary teacher

Gary Stidder and Andy Davies

INTRODUCTION

The aim of this chapter is to give you an insight into the demands of learning to teach in the professional environment of a secondary school. Teaching is a profession that is largely learned 'on the job' and this means that expectations will be high from the start and rightly so; while you can improve as a teacher, pupils only have one chance at each year of school. In a 2013 MORI opinion poll teachers were ranked the second most trusted professionals next to medical doctors, with bankers and politicians ranked as the least trusted. Being a teacher, therefore, requires individuals who are committed and understand the significance of this privileged position in society.

Chapter 3 detailed a range of different pathways to achieve QTS. Regardless of which pathway you might follow there is an expectation that all entrants to the profession successfully complete a minimum of 120 days of training in two contrasting schools (DfE, 2015). Within this chapter the processes and challenges of successfully completing school-based training is described in two main sections.

1. Firstly, the Teachers' Standards (DfE, 2013) that currently define what it means to be an effective teacher are introduced. This section explains the demands of these standards, highlighting the importance of the second part related to professionalism and the meaning of this within a secondary context.

2. Secondly, the reflective practice model of professional learning that is the dominant approach in most ITE courses is presented. This is explored through a review of the processes of subject mentor support for student teachers, the place of academic study and the issue of workload management.

THE TEACHERS' STANDARDS

The Teachers' Standards *'define the minimum level of practice expected of trainees and teachers from the point of being awarded QTS'* (DfE, 2012). In order to achieve QTS, student teachers need to demonstrate that they have shown the ability to meet these descriptions of what a teacher should be able to achieve.

Professional standards are therefore of great importance and as such are highly politicised. The first set of centrally agreed standards for teachers was introduced in 1998 by the Teacher Training Agency (TTA, 1997) as an attempt to ensure consistently high standards in ITE and to promote ongoing professional development as a requirement for all qualified teachers. Through successive versions of the Teachers' Standards, the choice of what aspects of teachers' work to include or exclude has been a controversial one as whatever is emphasised plays an important role in influencing what teachers actually do and how they are judged as being successful or not (Lawlor, 2004).

Whether or not someone should be awarded QTS is normally assessed through a range of means: observations of teaching practice; review of the impact of teaching on pupil progress; and academic work which is often collated in a portfolio of evidence (eg samples of work by pupils, lesson plan proformas, feedback on lesson observations) put together by student teachers themselves. When working towards 'meeting' the Teachers' Standards, student teachers bring a variety of experiences and knowledge: previous education, professional experience, interests and hobbies, experience as learners, any academic work they complete during their training course and time spent in a professional setting observing and working with experienced colleagues.

Research focus

Goepel, J (2012) Upholding Public Trust: An Examination of Teacher Professionalism and the Use of Teachers' Standards in England. *Teacher Development: An International Journal of Teachers' Professional Development*, 16(4): 489–505.

Janet Goepel takes a critical view of the current Teachers' Standards. In this article she presents an account of the development of the current Teachers' Standards and argues that their definition of what it is to be a professional teacher is a limited one. Goepel asserts that the standards are a list of easily '*assessable ... expected behaviours*' (p 500) in which professionalism is equated with government control over education rather than allowing creativity and the freedom to develop new approaches to teaching and schooling.

Understanding the Teachers' Standards

The Teachers' Standards are presented in two sections: Part One outlines eight 'Standards for Teaching' while Part Two describes the 'Standards for Personal and Professional Conduct' (DfE, 2013). The Teachers' Standards (see Appendix) are reproduced below with brief guidance explaining how these can be addressed in a secondary classroom. The guidance is developed from the National Association of School-Based Teacher Trainers' (NASBTT) (2015) *Training and Assessment Toolkit* that has been developed by different ITE providers with input from Ofsted officials. While it is certainly the case that the Teachers' Standards do not describe all aspects of work you might be involved in as a teacher, an understanding of them is important to give an insight into the demands of the profession.

Part One: Teaching

A teacher must:

Teachers' Standard 1: Set high expectations which inspire, motivate and challenge pupils

○ *establish a safe and stimulating environment for pupils, rooted in mutual respect;*

○ *set goals that stretch and challenge pupils of all backgrounds, abilities and dispositions;*

○ *demonstrate consistently the positive attitudes, values and behaviour which are expected of pupils.*

As a secondary teacher this means using a range of strategies to create a well-ordered and engaging teaching environment. There is also an emphasis on including and challenging all pupils to achieve the best possible outcomes. Additionally, the importance of being a good role model as a teacher is highlighted here as the basis for excellent classroom and behaviour management.

Teachers' Standard 2: Promote good progress and outcomes by pupils

○ *be accountable for pupils' attainment, progress and outcomes;*

○ *be aware of pupils' capabilities and their prior knowledge, and plan teaching to build on these;*

○ *guide pupils to reflect on the progress they have made and their emerging needs;*

○ *demonstrate knowledge and understanding of how pupils learn and how this impacts on teaching;*

○ *encourage pupils to take a responsible and conscientious attitude to their own work and study.*

Teachers' Standard 2 emphasises that teachers need to take responsibility for the progress and outcomes of all the pupils they work with. Teachers are meant to keep detailed ongoing records of pupils' achievements and use these to build on pupils' strengths and areas for development. There is also an expectation here that as education professionals, teachers understand the learning process and use this knowledge productively within their teaching.

Teachers' Standards 3: Demonstrate good subject and curriculum knowledge

○ *have a secure knowledge of the relevant subject(s) and curriculum areas, foster and maintain pupils' interest in the subject, and address misunderstandings;*

○ *demonstrate a critical understanding of developments in the subject and curriculum areas, and promote the value of scholarship;*

○ *demonstrate an understanding of and take responsibility for promoting high standards of literacy, articulacy and the correct use of standard English, whatever the teacher's specialist subject;*

○   *if teaching early reading, demonstrate a clear understanding of systematic synthetic phonics;*

○   *if teaching early mathematics, demonstrate a clear understanding of appropriate teaching strategies.*

The importance of holding excellent knowledge of your specialist subject and understanding its place in the curriculum is promoted in this standard. As a secondary teacher, the expectation that you will continue to be a scholar of your specialist area throughout your career is an important one. Despite the significance of subject specialism it is important to note that all teachers play a critical role in developing pupils' spoken and written literacy. The final two points covering early reading and early mathematics are more related to the demands for primary teachers but are worth acknowledging as secondary teachers are expected to build upon the skills and knowledge developed by colleagues in other phases.

Teachers' Standard 4: Plan and teach well-structured lessons

○   *impart knowledge and develop understanding through effective use of lesson time;*

○   *promote a love of learning and children's intellectual curiosity;*

○   *set homework and plan other out-of-class activities to consolidate and extend the knowledge and understanding pupils have acquired;*

○   *reflect systematically on the effectiveness of lessons and approaches to teaching;*

○   *contribute to the design and provision of an engaging curriculum within the relevant subject area(s).*

The focus here is on the importance of enabling pupils to access and engage with a subject over both the short term (individual lessons) and the longer term (ie within a 'scheme of work' covering a series of lessons). Creating and teaching exciting and engaging lessons is defined here as 'imparting' knowledge – synonymous with 'passing on' knowledge – promoting teacher talk. At the same time, teachers are also expected to find ways to inspire curiosity and promote a love of learning. This is also connected to the importance of setting meaningful and challenging homework that develops the learning that takes place in the lessons. A key element of this standard is the duty of teachers to practise ongoing reflection on the success of their teaching and then amending planning, as appropriate, from this.

Teachers' Standard 5: Adapt teaching to respond to the strengths and weaknesses of all pupils

○   *know when and how to differentiate appropriately, using approaches which enable pupils to be taught effectively;*

○   *have a secure understanding of how a range of factors can inhibit pupils' ability to learn, and how best to overcome these;*

○   *demonstrate an awareness of the physical, social and intellectual development of children, and know how to adapt teaching to support pupils' education at different stages of development;*

○   *have a clear understanding of the needs of all pupils, including those with special educational needs; those of high ability; those with English as an additional language; those with disabilities and be able to use and evaluate distinctive teaching approaches to engage and support them.*

The principle of including all pupils regardless of their learning needs, background or prior attainment is enshrined in international law and is essential for the education and life-chances of young people. This standard builds on Teachers' Standard 2 as it is concerned with the process of ensuring that all pupils make good progress through teaching to their specific strengths and specific needs. Adapting teaching by changing tasks, varying support materials or even giving more teacher support is known as *differentiation*. This is an important skill to develop and it is built on knowledge of the individual pupils you work with, knowledge of potential barriers to learning pupils can face, and also a sharp understanding of strategies that support different groups of learners (eg pupils with dyslexia or pupils who are judged to be of high ability) and how these can be used sensitively.

Teachers' Standard 6: Make accurate and productive use of assessment

○   *know and understand how to assess the relevant subject and curriculum areas, including statutory assessment requirements;*

○   *make use of formative and summative assessment to secure pupils' progress;*

○   *use relevant data to monitor progress, set targets, and plan subsequent lessons;*

○   *give pupils regular feedback, both orally and through accurate marking, and encourage pupils to respond to the feedback.*

High quality ongoing assessment of pupils with clear feedback that focuses on improving performance has been identified as having the biggest impact on learning of any intervention strategy (Hattie, 2012). This standard promotes the objective of developing secure knowledge of how to assess learning, how to record such assessments, and how to use this to inform teaching and learning. Within this standard there is also a focus on the increasing demand for teachers to be able to interpret and apply data held by schools to support pupils' progress and outcomes.

Teachers' Standard 7: Manage behaviour effectively to ensure a good and safe learning environment

○   *have clear rules and routines for behaviour in classrooms, and take responsibility for promoting good and courteous behaviour both in classrooms and around the school, in accordance with the school's behaviour policy;*

○   *have high expectations of behaviour, and establish a framework for discipline with a range of strategies, using praise, sanctions and rewards consistently and fairly;*

○   *manage classes effectively, using approaches which are appropriate to pupils' needs in order to involve and motivate them;*

○   *maintain good relationships with pupils, exercise appropriate authority, and act decisively when necessary.*

This standard seeks to guide teachers on core principles to support the creation of an excellent climate for learning. Every school you might work in has its own policy for behaviour and this will outline the rules and routines that are used as well as the sanctions when these are not adhered to. A key element of this standard is the importance of seeking to prevent behaviour becoming a problem; the use of praise and rewards, as well as seeking to motivate pupils to be fully involved in lessons through creating engaging lessons are advocated.

Teachers' Standard 8: Fulfil wider professional responsibilities

o   *make a positive contribution to the wider life and ethos of the school;*

o   *develop effective professional relationships with colleagues, knowing how and when to draw on advice and specialist support;*

o   *deploy support staff effectively;*

o   *take responsibility for improving teaching through appropriate professional development, responding to advice and feedback from colleagues;*

o   *communicate effectively with parents with regard to pupils' achievements and well-being.*

Being an effective teacher is about more than the work that takes place in classrooms and when supervising pupils at breaks. As a professional you will be a member of a wider team with responsibilities to your colleagues and the community you work with. Teachers are expected to engage with parents and also to work collaboratively with other professionals to support learning and meet individual pupil needs. At the same time there is an expectation of taking responsibility for your own professional development that relates to the reflective practitioner model that is discussed below.

Part Two: Personal and professional conduct

o   *Teachers uphold public trust in the profession and maintain high standards of ethics and behaviour, within and outside school, by:*

　　o   *treating pupils with dignity, building relationships rooted in mutual respect, and at all times observing proper boundaries appropriate to a teacher's professional position;*

　　o   *having regard for the need to safeguard pupils' well-being, in accordance with statutory provisions;*

　　o   *showing tolerance of and respect of the rights of others;*

　　o   *not undermining fundamental British values, including democracy, the rule of law, individual liberty and mutual respect, and tolerance of those with different faiths and beliefs;*

　　o   *ensuring that personal beliefs are not expressed in ways which exploit pupils' vulnerability or might lead them to break the law.*

○ *Teachers must have proper and professional regard for the ethos, policies and practices of the school in which they teach, and maintain high standards in their own attendance and punctuality.*

○ *Teachers must have an understanding of, and always act within, the statutory frameworks which set out their professional duties and responsibilities.*

Part Two of the Teachers' Standards relates to the personal and professional conduct that student and qualified teachers are expected to demonstrate at all times. From our point of view as tutors in ITE we would emphasise that the following elements of professional behaviour are especially important to know about for anyone considering getting into secondary teaching.

○ **Punctuality**: Within schools teachers are expected to act as role models for pupils by arriving well before the start of lessons to ensure the maximum time for learning is realised. It is normal practice for teachers to arrive prior to the start of the school day and to stay after lessons end to complete planning and marking and to meet with colleagues as scheduled.

○ **Attendance**: Teachers are not able to take leave during term time except in exceptional circumstances. When absence cannot be avoided (such as illness) there is an expectation that teachers will set work for whoever is asked to cover their lessons.

○ **Professional appearance**: The expectation that teachers act as role models extends to their appearance and there is increasing emphasis placed on the importance of secondary teachers dressing in a formal 'business-like' manner.

○ **Use of social media**: All teachers need to be aware of the appropriate use of social media, both within the school setting and in their own time. It is essential to ensure that any use of social media does not compromise your professional role.

○ **Confidentiality and privacy**: As a professional you would be privy to information about pupils and colleagues that is not to be shared with other people. Teachers need to take care to pay respect to the privacy and dignity of others.

○ **Professional relationships with colleagues**: Treating colleagues with respect in any form of communication is of great importance in any profession and is of particular significance in the busy and fast-moving environment of a secondary school.

Part Two of the Teachers' Standards also states the importance of ensuring 'British values' are not undermined. Clarification in support materials by the Department for Education (DfE, 2014) defines this as paying respect to all individuals and groups of people and actively combating discrimination. Finally, and perhaps most importantly, the demands related to safeguarding pupils by paying attention to child protection issues are specified in Part Two of the Teachers' Standards. Within any ITE pathway and also when being inducted into a school you will be introduced to your responsibilities in this area and it is essential that you are confident about understanding and applying such policies.

Student teacher voice

What strategies do you recommend to meet the Teachers' Standards?

During an ITE programme it is normal to collect evidence of how you have met the Standards for teaching and personal and professional conduct. James and Maria discuss the advice they would give to others having successfully done this.

James: *Setting weekly targets with my subject mentor enabled me to break down each teaching standard. I was able to find small pieces of evidence on a weekly basis which I collected in my portfolio of evidence. This enabled me to identify areas or particular teaching standards which required a greater amount of evidence.*

Maria: *I wish I had taken advice from my tutors and been organised from the start of the year! Making copies of evidence from the start and keeping a careful record of them is of great importance. It certainly takes longer to find things later on than it does to do this little and often.*

Reflective task

The Teachers' Standards are often referred to during interviews for ITE courses.

o   What knowledge, experience and skills do you hold that relate to the different Standards explained above? (eg have you experience of managing behaviour in a youth club or of fulfilling professional responsibilities in a job?)

o   Which ones do you think you would need the most support with?

There is no one correct answer that is being sought if you are asked such questions. What is important is to share an honest assessment of your strengths and areas for development as the capacity to be a 'reflective practitioner' is prized in teaching.

REFLECTIVE PRACTICE AND LEARNING TO TEACH

While reflective practice has been critiqued as a *'fuzzy concept'*, interpreted in ITE in a wide variety of ways (Collin et al, 2013, p 109), there is general agreement about its nature. Moon (1999) refers to reflective practice as the skill of being able to look at your own professional activity and then think about what you do, why you do it and ways of developing it in a systematic and evidence-informed way.

Boud et al (1985, p 34) believe this process is worthwhile because:

> The outcomes of reflection may include a new way of doing something, the clarification of an issue, the development of a skill or the resolution of a problem.

Since teachers continually face new challenges brought by new pupils, curricula, policies and technologies, the ability to solve one's own problems through reflective practice is of significance. From the mid-1990s the dominance of the reflective practitioner model of professional learning has been almost total in English ITE (Collin et al, 2013). A key author in the field of reflective practice is Donald Schön.

Research focus

Schön, D (1983) *The Reflective Practitioner: How Professionals Think in Action.* USA: Basic Books.

In the above book Schön outlines his conception of professional learning through reflective practice. This can be summarised as '*the capacity to reflect on action so as to engage in a process of continuous learning*' (Schön, 1983, p 68). He uses the following two concepts to explain how it can lead to professional expertise.

○ **Reflection-on-action**: this occurs after an activity and involves a commitment to spending time evaluating what happened. Through this process professionals develop new ways of approaching their work.

○ **Reflection-in-action**: this occurs while involved in an activity and is often characterised as the ability to 'think on your feet'. Schön argues this ability is developed through amassing a repertoire of experience and prior knowledge that can be drawn upon to respond to different professional challenges.

Reflection and reflexivity

The concept of *reflexivity* is often referred to in discussions of reflective practice as a way to enhance the quality of reflective practice. Reflexivity has been defined as:

> an ability to recognize our own influence – and the influence of our social and cultural contexts on research, the type of knowledge we create, and the way we create it … In this sense, it is about factoring ourselves as players into the situations we practice in.

> (Fook and Askeland, 2006, p 45)

While reflective practice focuses on learning from professional activity, reflexivity emphasises the importance of our own beliefs and actions in the type of professional activity we become involved in. Advocates of this model of reflective practice argue that developing the ability to be reflective and reflexive comes from committing to practising it. Taking time to reflect-on-action by thinking, writing, discussing issues with peers and colleagues and researching key issues are common ways that your ITE course will maximise your opportunities to be reflective and reflexive.

Two student teachers, Lily and Hannah, share their experiences of reflection and why they found it such a powerful mechanism for learning.

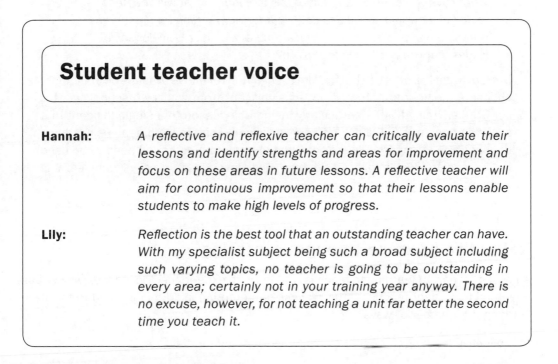

Student teacher voice

Hannah: *A reflective and reflexive teacher can critically evaluate their lessons and identify strengths and areas for improvement and focus on these areas in future lessons. A reflective teacher will aim for continuous improvement so that their lessons enable students to make high levels of progress.*

Lily: *Reflection is the best tool that an outstanding teacher can have. With my specialist subject being such a broad subject including such varying topics, no teacher is going to be outstanding in every area; certainly not in your training year anyway. There is no excuse, however, for not teaching a unit far better the second time you teach it.*

Reflective task

When supporting the student teachers we work with to engage in reflective practice, we often use the three questions and prompts below that are influenced by the work of Moon (1999, 2013) and Bolton (2014). While on teaching practice the student teachers are asked to identify one significant learning moment from the previous week and write up to 500 words about it to reflect-on-action.

1. **What happened**?

   Describe the significant learning moment. What made it important to you? How did you feel about it? What influence did you have on the events?

2. **What made it significant?**

   Why and how was it significant for you? Was there anything surprising about it? How does it connect to research, theory and policy in education you have come across elsewhere?

3. **What next**?

   What have you done as a result of this moment? What will you need to do? What would you like to do? What further reading and research will you engage in? Are there ethical /moral / political / wider social issues that you would like to explore?

In order to get a flavour of what it is like to engage in reflective practice on education, choose a memory that stands out as significant from your own schooling. This could be anything from a particularly memorable lesson to a single incident that sticks in your mind. Reflect on your significant learning moment using these questions and prompts. Please note that the prompts do not all need to be used but instead are designed as aids to help you to investigate the significant learning moment.

Reflective practice through mentoring

An essential part of learning to teach is working with experienced colleagues who act as 'mentors' to student teachers. The process of mentoring in ITE is intended to facilitate learning in a number of ways:

- reflective learning through providing opportunities for dialogue;
- coaching provided by an experienced expert teacher;
- the mentor acting as a role model who exemplifies good professional practice.

The mentor is a key person with whom student teachers have the most daily contact during their school-based training.

Mentoring is regarded as a core professional development activity for all members of the teaching profession. This person is typically an experienced teacher who wants to work with student teachers. They can be extremely supportive and willing to share ideas and experiences. Often one of the major constraints faced by teachers is lack of time, so student teachers need to be flexible and able to use time efficiently. Different ITE courses have different arrangements for mentor support but often a timetabled meeting slot is arranged to discuss progress and action plans. Mentors will normally create a suitably varied timetable of classes so that student teachers experience teaching a range of age groups, abilities and class sizes. Mentors check lesson plans and observe lessons on a regular basis, providing clear feedback and suggesting areas for development and ways forward to improve lessons. They are likely to observe you both informally and formally and write about your ability to meet the teaching standards required in order to achieve QTS.

To support mentors, tutors from ITE providers will visit student teachers while in school. These visits may have different purposes and foci but the overall emphasis will always be on supporting your progress and liaising with the school to ensure that the training is of a high standard.

Beulah, Robert and Sam are three student teachers who share their thoughts on the importance of the mentoring process in learning to teach.

Student teacher voice

What is the value of having an effective mentor during your school-based training?

Beulah: *A great mentor to me is someone who wants to support a student teacher to become his or her best. They've been a student teacher themselves so understand how daunting it can feel and therefore show support by supporting your learning, just like you do for the pupils. They're approachable, organised and get to know you. They give personal stepping stones to aid you to become the best teacher you can be with realistic challenges. They are great role models and can show you what an outstanding lesson looks like.*

Robert: *Without a mentor, the reflective process of building subject knowledge and mastering your practice would be very difficult. An effective mentor is one who guides your development while nurturing your confidence. A good mentor will develop a reflective teacher and see mistakes or bad lessons as a way to improve.*

Sam: *A mentor enables a student teacher to make progress, building confidence and competence. An effective mentor will set targets which are specific and appropriate for the student teacher. An effective mentor also provides increasing levels of independence when it is appropriate to enable them to have a realistic experience of being a qualified teacher.*

Academic study and reflective practice

Most if not all pathways that lead to the award of QTS contain academic study elements that are designed to complement and enhance school-based training. The form of this academic study differs (covering, for example, written essays, mini-research projects, presentations and oral exams) but all will be based on an expectation of engaging with and/or producing rigorously researched, carefully structured and well-argued work.

The place of academic study in learning to teach has been an area of ongoing controversy, some arguing that theory has no place in the practice-based profession of teaching. Such debates can even be traced back as far as the start of organised teacher training in this country at the start of the nineteenth century (Dent, 1977)! However, we would argue that engagement in academic work as part of learning to teach can be of significant use for the following reasons.

○   Different courses structure academic study so that it complements and develops classroom practice and expertise. Such work will normally be carefully designed to help you to meet the Teachers' Standards.

○   Academic assignments facilitate the development of a critical appreciation of the field of education. As Eales-Reynolds et al (2013) assert, engagement in focused reading and writing can help you to adopt a way of thinking that enables you to think objectively and innovatively about difficult situations and issues.

○   As well as enabling you to see what works in education, academic study should allow you to identify what Adey and Dillon (2012) class as *'bad education'* (p xii). Unhelpful practices such as 'neuromyths' and 'learning styles' are common in schools despite having no basis in evidence or any beneficial impact on pupil learning.

○   Academic study is an ongoing expectation for qualified teachers in Teachers' Standard 8 (*'take responsibility for improving teaching through appropriate professional development'*). It is helpful as a way to enable fresh approaches and development throughout your teaching career.

○   Reflective practice learning is made rigorous when backed by reference to a wider and credible evidence base. As part of the process of reflection-on-action, engagement with a range of evidence ensures that decisions about practice are based on solid foundations rather than what could possibly be the whims of an individual.

Two student teachers, Kirit and Felicity, share their thoughts on the place of academic assignments in learning to teach.

Student teacher voice

Kirit: *Academic assignments provide the structure to your practice, and well planned essays from your university on topics such as assessment and differentiation can help you develop your teaching while on placement.*

Felicity: *Assignments ensure that teachers are up to date with research in their subject area. I found the assignments beneficial as I had an opportunity to justify why my subject should be in the curriculum. The assignments also involved designing teaching resources and investigating different methods of assessment which I was able to apply in my lessons during my teaching placements.*

Reflective task

When deciding which ITE course to select, research the following issues.

o   What kind of assignments do different courses offer? (ie is there a mixture of different types?)

o   What kind of support is offered to complete them?

o   How are they designed to complement student teachers' ongoing development during and after the course?

WORKLOAD MANAGEMENT

A common concern of teachers, as discussed in Chapter 2, is the heavy workload and the impact it can have on the effectiveness of teachers and their well-being. At the time of writing, reviews are taking place into the issue and Education Secretary Nicky Morgan has pledged to cut teachers' workloads, not least due to the negative impact this is believed to have on recruitment to the profession (Coughlan, 2014). The teaching union National Association of Schoolmasters / Union of Women Teachers (NASUWT) has produced guidance (NASUWT, 2011), as has *The Guardian's Teacher Network* (Marsh, 2014), to support the workload of teachers, which would be relevant to take note of during an ITE programme.

o   Ask for help if facing difficulties and make people aware if you believe you are working excessive hours per week. For a student teacher, help can come from mentors and staff from the ITE course you are following.

o   Talk to colleagues about the strategies they use to work as efficiently and effectively as possible.

o   Be mindful of the additional time commitment of extra-curricular activities.

o   Maintain outside interests and exercise regularly.

o   Seek to maintain separation between work and home by completing work on site.

CONCLUSION

The aim of this chapter was to support you with your decision about whether to get into secondary teaching by examining the nature of professional learning for secondary school teaching. While learning to teach in a secondary school is a significant task and an important responsibility, it is worth remembering that courses are carefully structured to scaffold the development of new teachers. The following progress checklist and the 'taking it further' section are intended to draw out the significance of reflective tasks and to highlight key works to deepen your understanding of the topics discussed in this chapter.

 Progress checklist

Reflective tasks

The tasks in this chapter should have helped you to reflect on the challenges of professional learning in meeting the Teachers' Standards as well as learning in a professional setting alongside academic study.

Next steps

You should now be in a position to research different ITE pathways and courses from the point of view of the type of professional learning they offer. We recommend thinking carefully about your preferences here and researching which options best fit your knowledge of yourself as a learner.

▶▶ **TAKING IT FURTHER**

Bolton, G (2014) *Reflective Practice: Writing and Professional Development.* 4th ed. London: Sage.

Provides a clear explanation of methods to use to engage in reflective practice. Theoretical models of reflective practice are explained with examples from practice through case studies.

Eales-Reynolds, L, Judge, B, McCreery, E and Jones, P (2013) *Critical Thinking Skills for Education Students.* 2nd ed. London: Learning Matters.

This text provides support for non-classroom-based aspects of ITE, helping the reader to examine, challenge and interpret the findings of educational research.

Pollard, A (2014) *Reflective Teaching in Schools.* 4th ed. London: Bloomsbury.

Provides support for professional learning as a secondary teacher on two levels: practical advice and classroom strategies are complemented by consideration of the evidence-informed principles and concepts that underpin effective practice.

Blogs and twitter feeds

Staffrm: http://staffrm.io/ (accessed 5 September 2015).

Staffrm is an online professional network for educators to share their professional learning and engage in discussion and debate. It is free to join and is designed to be easily accessible from smartphones as well as PCs.

Researched: @researchED1

Aims to raise research literacy in the teaching profession.

Teacher Support: @teachersupport

Independent charity providing emotional and practical support for teachers.

REFERENCES

Adey, P and Dillon, J (2012) Introduction, in Adey, P and Dillon, J (eds) *Bad Education: Debunking Myths in Education*. Maidenhead: Open University Press.

Bolton, G (2014) *Reflective Practice: Writing and Professional Development*. 4th ed. London: Sage.

Boud, D, Keogh, R and Walker, D (1985) Promoting Reflection in Learning: A Model, in Boud, D, Keogh, R and Walker, D (eds) *Reflection: Turning Experience into Learning*. Abingdon: Routledge.

Bryan, H, Carpenter, C and Hoult, S (2010) *Learning and Teaching at M-Level: A Guide for Student Teachers*. London: Sage.

Collin, S, Karsenti, T and Komis, V (2013) Reflective Practice in Initial Teacher Training: Critiques and Perspectives. *Reflective Practice: International and Multidisciplinary Perspectives*, 14(1): 104–17.

Coughlan, S (2014) Nicky Morgan pledges to reduce teacher workload, *BBC News*. [online] Available at: www.bbc.co.uk/news/education-29427844 (accessed 30 July 2015).

Dent, H (1977) *The Training of Teachers in England and Wales, 1800–1975*. London: Hodder and Stoughton.

Department for Education (DfE) (2013) *Teachers' Standards: Guidance for School Leaders, School Staff and Governing Bodies (Introduction updated June 2013).* London: Department for Education.

Department for Education (DfE) (2014) *Promoting Fundamental British Values as Part of SMSC in Schools: Departmental Advice for Maintained Schools.* London: Department for Education.

Department for Education (DfE) (2015) *Initial Teacher Training Criteria: Statutory Guidance for Accredited Initial Teacher Training Providers.* London: Department for Education.

Fook, J and Askeland, G (2006) Critical Reflection: A Review of Contemporary Literature and Understandings, in White, S, Fook, J and Gardner, F (eds) *Critical Reflection in Health and Social Care.* Maidenhead: Open University Press.

Goepel, J (2012) Upholding Public Trust: An Examination of Teacher Professionalism and the Use of Teachers' Standards in England. *Teacher Development*, 16(4): 489–505.

Hattie, J (2012) *Visible Learning for Teaching: Maximising Impact on Learning.* Abingdon: Routledge.

Lawlor, H (2004) The Role of the Teacher Training Agency: The First Set of National Standards, in Green, H (ed) *Professional Standards for Teachers and School Leaders: A Key to School Improvement.* Abingdon: RoutledgeFalmer.

Marsh, S (2014) Top 10 tips on how teachers improve their work-life balance, *The Guardian.* [online] Available at: www.theguardian.com/teacher-network/2014/dec/10/ten-tips-teachers-worklife-balance (accessed 1 October 2014).

Moon, J (1999) *Reflection in Learning and Professional Development.* Abingdon: RoutledgeFalmer.

Moon, J (2013) *A Handbook of Reflective and Experiential Learning: Theory and Practice.* Abingdon: RoutledgeFalmer.

MORI (2013) *Politicians Trusted Less than Estate Agents, Bankers and Journalists.* [online] Available at: www.ipsosmori.com/researchpublications/researcharchive/3133/Politicians-trusted-less-than-estate-agents-bankers-and-journalists.aspx (accessed 20 March 2015).

NASBTT (2015) *Training and Assessment Toolkit: A Guide to Accuracy in the Assessment of Trainees.* London: The National Association of School-Based Teacher Trainers.

NASUWT (2011) *Managing Your Health and Wellbeing: NASUWT Advice to Teachers and School Leaders.* [online] Available at: www.nasuwt.org.uk/consum/groups/public/@journalist/documents/nas_download/nasuwt_007706.pdf (accessed 5 September 2014).

Schön, D (1983) *The Reflective Practitioner: How Professionals Think in Action.* Boston: Arena Publishing.

Teacher Training Agency (TTA) (1997) *Standards for the Award of Qualified Teacher Status.* London: Teacher Training Agency.

Developing as a subject specialist

Brian Marsh and Chris Sweeney

INTRODUCTION

This chapter discusses one of the most essential features needed to be an excellent secondary teacher: subject knowledge. As Allison and Tharby (2015) astutely point out, teachers need a high level of subject knowledge if they are going to inspire, stretch and challenge pupils. This is backed up by a recent major review of research findings (Coe et al, 2014) that emphasises that a teacher's subject knowledge is directly related to their pupils' achievement.

The ways in which you acquire your subject knowledge will be as individual as you are. We believe that as you read this chapter you will gain a better understanding of what subject knowledge is and how you can go about enhancing your existing knowledge in order to make your application for teacher training more likely to succeed.

Teacher voice

Why is subject knowledge so important?

Robert: *Having a good level of subject knowledge is important as it allows me to make connections within my subject, as well as to other subjects beyond what I teach.*

Lou: *I teach a subject which is not my specialism. It takes longer to prepare and I am not as confident in front of the students as I am teaching my subject specialism.*

Reflective task

- As you begin the process of applying to become a teacher, reflect on why you are passionate about the subject you want to teach.

- What aspects of your subject do you feel are most important?

WHAT IS A SUBJECT SPECIALIST?

The importance of subject knowledge to the development of high quality teachers has already been stated; however, the definition of a subject specialist in school is complex. In the UK, the National Foundation for Educational Research (NFER, 2006) defines a *subject specialist* as:

o   someone who has studied that subject and has qualifications to degree level or above, or;

o   has undertaken training in that subject during their ITE programme.

While applicants to postgraduate ITE programmes to become secondary teachers do not have to have a degree directly applicable to their chosen subject area, it is a common expectation that they will.

WHAT IS SUBJECT KNOWLEDGE?

The third Teachers' Standard defines a necessary area of competence for all teachers as being able to '*demonstrate good subject and curriculum knowledge*' (see Appendix). This phrase can be understood in a number of different ways but we believe the following are important elements:

o   having robust subject knowledge for teaching;

o   an understanding of new developments in the subject;

o   the ability to identify and address pupil misconceptions;

o   use of the core skills of literacy and numeracy within the subject;

o   a commitment to ongoing scholarship within the subject area.

Research focus

Grossman, P L, Wilson, S M and Shulman, L S (1989) Teachers of Substance: Subject Matter Knowledge for Teaching, in Reynolds, M C (ed) *Knowledge Base for the Beginning Teacher*. New York: Pergamon.

Subject knowledge is clearly not a simple single idea; Grossman et al (1989) consider subject knowledge as having four dimensions. This is modelled in Figure 6.1:

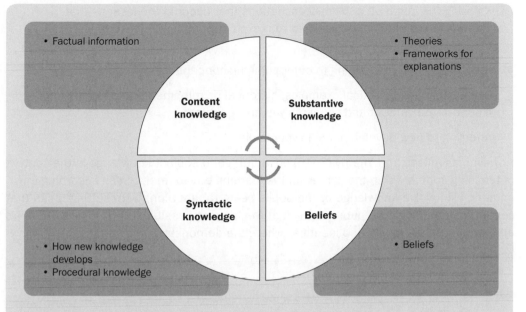

- Factual information
- Theories
- Frameworks for explanations
- How new knowledge develops
- Procedural knowledge
- Beliefs

Content knowledge

Substantive knowledge

Syntactic knowledge

Beliefs

Figure 6.1 The components of subject knowledge (adapted from Grossman et al (1989)

According to Grossman et al's model, as a subject specialist in school you will need to develop:

o a detailed factual knowledge of your subject;

o a deep understanding of the theories within your subject along with the frameworks for explaining those theories. This is important for being able to respond to pupil difficulties and misconceptions when learning the subject;

o an understanding of how new knowledge in the subject evolves and develops;

o personal beliefs about the subject matter such as why the subject matters.

Grossman et al's framework reinforces the understanding that subject knowledge for teaching involves more than having an accumulation of facts. It also includes you as a teacher having a good understanding of the theoretical side of your subject as well as developing frameworks for being able to explain the subject.

HOW DO TEACHERS DEMONSTRATE GOOD SUBJECT KNOWLEDGE?

There are a number of ways through which you will be able to demonstrate good subject knowledge. These include:

o being able to make the content real, relevant and applicable to the pupils you are teaching;

o knowing the common pupil misconceptions that occur in the lessons that you teach and planning to scaffold your explanations to minimise those misconceptions;

o recognising and responding to other pupil misconceptions in your lessons;

o using analogies, practical examples, historical developments and stories to illustrate the content and concepts you are teaching;

o referring to new developments in your subject.

However, as Allison and Tharby (2015) point out, good subject knowledge in the context of teaching comes within the context of the learning environment. Such a learning environment will involve knowledge of the pupils being taught along with setting tasks that continually challenge the pupils to think at the highest possible levels. Figure 6.2 is an adaptation of their model and identifies where the demonstration of good subject knowledge has the greatest impact.

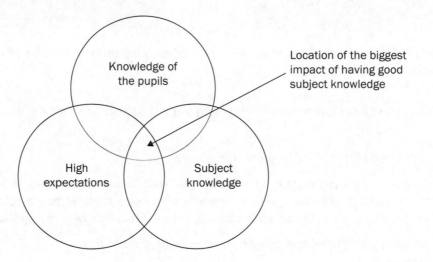

Figure 6.2 Where good subject knowledge is most effective (adapted from Allison and Tharby, 2015)

However, having well-developed knowledge of your subject does not necessarily mean that you will translate it into good teaching. Lock et al (2011) note that:

> a graduate of a particular subject is only likely to start their transformation into a teacher of that subject when they begin to consider how best to teach the subject content in order to make it learnable by others.
>
> (Lock et al, 2011, p 7)

It is this that Lee Shulman (1987) identified as *pedagogical content knowledge*, often referred to as PCK. What Shulman recognised was that if teachers are to be effective practitioners they need both in-depth knowledge of their subject and comprehensive knowledge and understanding of how to represent this subject knowledge and make it accessible to learners (Van Driel et al, 1998).

REVIEWING AND DEVELOPING SUBJECT KNOWLEDGE

A characteristic of good teachers is the way they take control of their own professional development, including developing their subject knowledge. In a number of countries (eg USA, Australia, England and Wales), teachers operate within a framework in which they have to teach a content-driven curriculum. In addition, many teachers, from those in initial training through to those with years of experience, find themselves teaching outside of their specialism (McCarthy and Youens, 2005).

In ITE you will be given strategies to support the development of your subject knowledge.

Subject audit

As part of the training process you will be asked to undertake an audit of your subject knowledge. This will take different forms depending upon your subject specialism but is important In determining the specific gaps in your subject knowledge for teaching. Such audits may include a demonstration of particular skills but sometimes consist of a written task such as a topic checklist or past examination questions. It is important here to recognise the limitations of the subject audit in this form. This is a self-assessment tool that records an individual's perception of their subject knowledge and in this sense might be seen as reinforcing the dislocation of subject knowledge and pedagogical content knowledge. The instrument used offers a *'limited list-like perspective of the knowledge held by a teacher'* (Prestage and Perks, 2001, p 102). The audit provides no information as to the depth of knowledge and understanding nor does it highlight any personally held misconceptions. In response to this, some subject associations are developing diagnostic subject audit materials.

Research focus

Kind, V and Taber, K (2005) *Science: Teaching School Subjects 11–19.* London: Routledge.

In this book, Kind and Taber identify two further related features that are required for effective subject teaching.

o   Breadth of subject knowledge – a subject-specific degree may not encompass all the detailed knowledge required in the school curriculum. Burn, Childs and McNicholl (2007) note that the content taught in history degrees may not bear much relationship to the content prescribed by the English national curriculum, for example.

o   Robustness of subject knowledge – preparing for degree-level examinations does not necessarily produce the familiar and thorough type of knowing required to teach. Being robust is about being very familiar with the subject so that you can teach it confidently in a variety of different contexts. This echoes the findings of Burn et al (2007), who found that beginning teachers experienced anxieties over subject knowledge, and Marsh and Mitchell (2010), where participants in subject knowledge development programmes spoke of the need to develop 'robust' subject knowledge and of their fears of 'not knowing the answer' when asked a question by pupils in the class.

An additional issue is that for a number of years it has been common for graduates with related degrees to enter the teaching profession. Examples are individuals with a degree in information technology applying for PGCE Computing, prospective teachers with degrees in engineering or accountancy applying for PGCE Mathematics and those with forensic science degrees applying for PGCE Chemistry. If this is similar to your background, a subject knowledge enhancement programme would be of real value.

Continuing subject knowledge development

While the subject knowledge audit will point to areas of subject content knowledge you will need to develop further, the research evidence points to the acquisition of this knowledge generally being either:

○ part of a teacher's planning – this occurs at the point where you may be asked to teach a lesson but find that the subject knowledge for that lesson is beyond your current level of knowledge. This is a deficit model and is a time-consuming and reactive process. A number of studies report teachers reacting to such a deficit by reading textbooks, drawing from detailed teaching schemes and reviewing online resources. A popular resource type, according to McCarthy and Youens (2005, p 157), is the use of revision guides because of 'their accessibility and value in indicating the level of content appropriate for pupils at different key stages';

○ through a specific training programme – pre- and post-ITE Subject Knowledge Enhancement (SKE) programmes and short subject-based courses are examples of this.

The challenge for the teacher, whether beginning or experienced, is to ensure the robustness of their subject knowledge, which implies a depth of both knowledge and understanding in the planning of immediately forthcoming lessons.

There are many ways in which teachers develop their subject knowledge. As you approach content that you will teach for the first time or which may even be outside of your specialism, it is likely that you will draw on one or more of the following methods to prepare for that lesson:

○ reflection on your own education and experience;

○ reading – usually related texts or teacher resource material;

○ web-based resources, eg TES;

○ material from your subject-specific professional associations;

○ using past examination questions along with the published markscheme. This, along with feedback from a trusted colleague, is invaluable for developing your subject knowledge;

○ continuing professional development (CPD) to develop your subject-specific knowledge, eg through examination boards or externally funded courses.

Keeping up to date with subject-specific knowledge also happens through informal ways. You can keep abreast of the latest developments in your subject through visits to art galleries and museums, by watching TV documentaries and reading magazines such as the Royal Geographical Society's monthly magazine *Geographical* or the *New Scientist*.

Traditionally, a teacher's subject knowledge has been seen as individualistic. However, a reading of Ellis (2007) suggests that subject knowledge has been historically developed through culturally significant practices, is relational in nature and is always accessed and developed within the existing social systems within which teachers practise. Secondary school teachers in England spend most of their time in subject departments – it is here where collective knowledge is developed (Hodkinson and Hodkinson, 2005). The shared expertise of more experienced teacher-colleagues cannot be overestimated.

You will find valuable support both from other student teachers and teachers in the subject departments when you begin your training. McCarthy and Youens (2005) reported that peer support within cohorts of student teachers was highly valued in subject knowledge development as it was interactive and collegial. This supports the findings of Lock et al (2011), who found that student teachers rate highly both peers and classroom teachers as being important for the development of subject knowledge and topic-specific pedagogy.

The importance of collegiality is supported in the literature. Youens and McCarthy (2007), for example, note that teachers themselves are a rich and useful source of knowledge about teaching. Much of this is spontaneous learning that arises at the point of need. An important feature in this is the use of dedicated departmental classrooms and offices, which are places where informal learning can take place.

Student teacher voice

How did you develop your subject knowledge as a student teacher?

Chris: *When I was due to teach a topic I wasn't sure of I would read about it in a textbook and then go and talk to one of the teachers in the department.*

Jenny:	*I would go online. I found that the BBC Bitesize website could help me start thinking about a subject area that was unknown to me.*
Julie:	*I found revision guides really useful in giving me a framework for what I was going to teach.*

The effects of not having good subject knowledge

Subject knowledge is identified as an important indicator of the quality of teaching. If you have a high level of specialised subject knowledge you will have:

○   a vast range of factual knowledge about your subject;

○   a deep understanding of the theoretical aspects of your subject;

○   a conceptual framework for organising your knowledge;

○   knowledge of the 'big ideas' in your subject;

○   a range of 'stories' about your specialist subject which aids the giving of explanations.

At the time of writing the current *School Inspection Handbook* (Ofsted, 2015, p 46) notes that outstanding teachers '... *demonstrate deep knowledge and understanding of the subjects they teach*'. Your depth of subject knowledge therefore has a clear impact on the quality of your teaching.

However, it is a different story if your subject knowledge is not strong. In a study carried out by McCarthy and Youens (2005), they identified a lack of robustness in the subject knowledge of student teachers. Further evidence comes from Richardson (2006), who observed that in some lessons, early career teachers' misunderstandings were evident and misconceptions expressed by pupils went unchallenged.

Sanders et al (1993), writing about experienced teachers, reported that teaching outside one's subject specialism appears to have an impact on the quality of lesson planning. Such issues include difficulties in structuring lessons, lack of confidence and depth when responding to pupils, lack of creativity and lack of challenge that extends the pupils' thinking and use of what they have learned in a lesson. The overall impact is a narrowing of the range of activities, analogies, models and illustrations that help develop pupil understanding. Consequently, lessons can become more rigid, constrained and less creative. Childs and McNicholl (2007) support this view and add the feature of selecting and using resources. Even with extensively resourced schemes of work, teachers operating outside their specialism can be disadvantaged by not having the specific subject knowledge to make an informed choice of resources.

Reflective task

- ○ Think back to some of the lessons you had at school where you struggled to understand what was being taught. Why do you think it was? Was it because the subject content was too difficult? Was it because of the way in which it was presented?

- ○ Now put yourself in the place of the teacher. How might you avoid the same thing happening in your classroom when you are teaching?

CONCLUSION

The importance of high quality subject knowledge cannot be overemphasised. The quality and depth of a teacher's subject knowledge makes a difference in personal practice and also pupil learning. It is from this that teachers, both beginning and experienced, have a well-developed understanding of the subject and comprehend the conceptual links and frameworks in that subject. They are able to recognise pupil misconceptions when they arise. Moreover, such teachers have a wealth of background information and anecdotes that illuminate their teaching. Teachers with stronger subject knowledge are more likely to ask more detailed questions, undertake a greater number of investigations and be more responsive to pupil questions. You will need to make sure that you observe teaching and learning taking place in education settings and think about how you could start to convert your subject knowledge into knowledge that your potential pupils will understand and learn from.

As we have said, it is not uncommon for many teachers to teach outside of their own subject specialism. Limitations in subject knowledge result in a more rigid and restrictive approach to teaching. Difficulties are experienced in planning a coherent conceptual storyline both within a lesson but also across a sequence of lessons. Questioning and discussion is much more limited and the ability to both identify and respond to pupil misconceptions is limited. For this group of teachers, strategies for developing subject knowledge are important. While there are formal mechanisms, eg pre- and post-ITE SKE programmes, in some subject areas, the importance of learning from colleagues cannot be overemphasised. This is a very powerful way of developing as a subject specialist.

It is necessary to reaffirm that high quality subject knowledge alone does not equate to high quality teaching. Teachers not only need to know what to teach but also need to know how to teach any particular topic. Developing your pedagogic content knowledge will be essential to ensuring that high quality pupil learning takes place in every one of your lessons.

Progress checklist

Reflective tasks

This chapter has explained the importance of having excellent subject knowledge, not just for yourself but for the pupils you will teach during your career. It has also given you ideas as to how you can improve your existing knowledge and develop it further. We have also explained what the potential difficulties are if your subject knowledge is weak.

Next steps

We would suggest that you review and study the examination syllabuses for your chosen subject, so that you can find out exactly what is being taught in secondary schools. These syllabuses (usually known as subject specifications) will also give you a chance to see what depth of knowledge you will be required to have when teaching GCSE or A level. The three main examination boards are AQA, OCR and EdExcel and their website details are listed here:

- www.aqa.org.uk

- www.edexcel.org.uk

- www.ocr.org.uk

▶▶ **TAKING IT FURTHER**

Blogs and twitter feeds

As a subject specialist it is helpful to keep up to date with the latest developments in education.

Institute of Education subject knowledge blog: https://ioelondonblog. wordpress.com/tag/subject-knowledge/ (accessed 1 October 2015).

Schools Week: @SchoolsWeek

Schools, Students and Teachers network (SSAT): @ssat

REFERENCES

Allison, S and Tharby, A (2015) *Making Every Lesson Count*. Camarthen: Crown House Publishing.

Burn, K, Childs, A and McNicholl, J (2007) The Potential and Challenges for Student Teachers' Learning of Subject-specific Pedagogical Knowledge within Secondary School Departments. *The Curriculum Journal*, 18(4): 429–45.

Burn, K, Mutton, T and Hagger, H (2007) *Learning from Experience: The Focus and Orientations of Beginning Teachers' Learning.* Paper presented at the British Educational Research Association Conference, London, August 2007.

Childs, A and McNicholl, J (2007) Investigating the Relationship between Subject Content Knowledge and Pedagogical Practice through the Analysis of Discourse. *International Journal of Science Education*, 29(13): 1629–53.

Coe, R, Aloisi, C, Higgins, S and Elliot Major, L (2014) *What Makes Great Teaching? Review of the Underpinning Research*. London: The Sutton Trust. Available at: www.suttontrust.com/researcharchive/great-teaching/ (accessed 2 October 2015).

Ellis, V (2007) Taking Subject Knowledge Seriously: From Professional Knowledge Recipes to Complex Conceptualisations of Teacher Development. *The Curriculum Journal*, 18(4): 447–62.

Grossman, P L, Wilson, S M and Shulman, L S (1989) Teachers of Substance: Subject Matter Knowledge for Teaching, in Reynolds, M C (ed) *Knowledge Base for the Beginning Teacher*. New York: Pergamon.

Hodkinson, H and Hodkinson, P (2005) Improving School Teachers' Workplace Learning. *Research Papers in Education*, 20(2): 109–31.

Kind, V and Taber, K (2005) *Science: Teaching School Subjects 11–19*. London: Routledge.

Lock, R, Salt, D and Soares, A (2011) *Trainee Science Teachers' Acquisition of Subject Knowledge and Pedagogy in One Year Postgraduate Initial Teacher Training Courses in England and Wales*. University of Birmingham. A report for the Wellcome Trust. [online] Available at: www.wellcome.ac.uk/About-us/Publications/Reports/Education/WTVM053203.htm (accessed 30 July 2015).

Marsh, B and Mitchell, N (2010) *The Use of Video in Developing the Subject Knowledge of Science Teachers*. Paper presented at ECER, Helsinki 25–27 August 2010.

McCarthy, S and Youens, B (2005) Strategies Used by Science Student Teachers for Subject Knowledge Development: A Focus on Peer Support. *Research in Science and Technological Education*, 23(2): 149–62.

National Foundation for Educational Research (NFER) (2006) *Mathematics and Science in Secondary Schools: The Deployment of Teachers and Support Staff to Deliver the Curriculum*. Research report no.708. NFER Trading Ltd.

Ofsted (2015) *School Inspection Handbook*. [online] Available from: www.gov.uk/government/publications/school-inspection-handbook-from-september-2015 (accessed 3 December 2015).

Prestage, S and Perks, P (2001) Models and Super-models: Ways of Thinking about Professional Knowledge in Mathematics Teaching, in Morgan, C and Jones, K (eds) *Research in Mathematics Education*. Vol. 3. London: British Research for Learning in Mathematics.

Richardson, I (2006) What is Good Science Education? in Wood-Robinson, V (ed) *ASE Guide to Science Education*. Hatfield: ASE.

Sanders, L, Borko, H and Lockard, J (1993) Secondary Science Teachers' Knowledge Base when Teaching Science Courses in and out of their Area of Certification. *Journal of Research in Science Teaching*, 30: 723–36.

Shulman, L (1987) Knowledge and Teaching: Foundations of the New Reform. *Harvard Educational Review*, 57: 1–22.

Van Driel, J, Verloop, N and De Vos, W (1998) Developing Science Teachers' Pedagogical Content Knowledge. *Journal of Research in Science Teaching*, 35: 673–95.

Classroom management

Sally Johnson and Sarah Poore

INTRODUCTION

Developing the essential skills of classroom management is one of the major areas of concern for student teachers, particularly at secondary level, and one of the main areas of focus during ITE.

This chapter focuses on the key elements and skills of classroom management. It considers the expectations and realities of life in the classroom. It looks at a variety of perspectives, including those of school staff, ITE tutors, pupils and parents and asks: What do these parties expect of you and where might you gain support in meeting their expectations? By examining what good classroom practice looks and feels like, some of the difficulties and challenges faced in the classroom, including behaviour management, are explored. There is also discussion of working with different groups of pupils and the ways in which teachers support the progress of all, through strategies such as differentiation and monitoring of progress data in order to develop an inclusive learning environment. Maintaining teacher well-being and a positive outlook are also considered.

In this chapter we share our beliefs and principles of classroom management drawn from our experience as classroom teachers, our work in ITE and CPD, and also our engagement with research in this field.

WHAT IS CLASSROOM MANAGEMENT?

Classroom management is a term used by teachers and the teaching profession to describe the complex process of ensuring that lessons run purposefully and productively. This covers a wide range of skills and techniques that teachers have to learn, practise and use effectively. A helpful discussion of the nature of classroom management is included in the research focus section below.

Research focus

Mundschenk, N, Milner, C and Nastally, B (2011) Effective Classroom Management: An Air Traffic Control Analogy. *Intervention in School and Clinic*, 47(2): 98–103.

Based on their experience as teacher educators in the United States, Mundschenk, Milner and Nastally developed the following definition and analogy to define classroom management and how it can be approached by practitioners.

1. **Classroom management definition**: this includes the rules and routines of the classroom, the physical environment, the way in which behaviour is managed and how learning is supported so all pupils are included.

2. **Classroom management analogy:** this analogy presents teachers as air traffic controllers and pupils as planes. It argues that the most effective classroom management is based on pupils taking responsibility for their learning and behaviour through the use of clearly articulated procedures that have been carefully planned in advance.

DEVELOPING CLASSROOM MANAGEMENT SKILLS

Managing expectations and what is expected of you

While contemplating a career in secondary teaching it is likely that you will visit different schools and departments to gain a flavour of the profession and experience different approaches in different settings. As noted elsewhere, it is a requirement of most ITE programmes that prospective student teachers have had secondary school observation experience. When you are training you will have experience of different placement settings and you will be working alongside a range of staff, pupils and parents.

It is worth considering that first impressions count and as a prospective teacher as soon as you walk into school your conduct and appearance will be noticed by all parties that you come into contact with, including pupils, parents, staff and others. It is a good idea to be aware of the school ethos, dress code and names and roles of personnel that you will be meeting. You need to set out clear expectations and lead by example. Do not expect instant respect by virtue of being a classroom teacher; it may take time, effort and consistency for positive relationships to develop. Respect has to be earned and reciprocated.

Reflective task

Consider each of the following scenarios and think how pupils, other teachers and parents might view these incidents. How might they impact on the way you are perceived by others?

o A pupil looks you up on social media and is able to view photographs and comments made by you and others.

o You attend a school performance one evening even though you had no part in the production.

o You participate in a weekend sporting tournament and do not have time to plan for your lessons on Monday.

○ You walk into the staffroom and overhear colleagues complaining about a particular pupil and their family. What they are saying is not pleasant.

○ You share some really helpful behaviour management ideas with another colleague.

At school the key professionals that you will be working closely with as a student teacher are the department and support staff, including your mentor. Everyone that you encounter will have expectations of you. Some of these are obvious and explicit while others can be equally important yet not clearly defined, as the following points illustrate.

Teacher voice

Jane is a mentor to student teachers in school:

I expect student teachers to be keen and enthusiastic and to show that they really want to work with our pupils ... I don't expect them to be a teacher straight away but want to see them willing to be brave and try new things. I love it when student teachers bring new ideas to the department! I also need them to be able to take constructive criticism in the way it is meant – to help them to become a really great teacher. I want them to recognise when they need help and to ask for it ... after all, we were all student teachers once!

Tutor voice

Sam is an ITE tutor:

I expect student teachers to be professional in everything they do – the way they work with colleagues and pupils, conduct themselves and organise themselves to make sure that they are planning and teaching clear and challenging lessons. I expect them to recognise that the university works together with the school as a partnership and that both components are important. I want to see well-organised student teachers committed to making learning inspirational.

Pupil voice

Ali is a Year 8 pupil:

It can be really good when you have a student teacher. I remember one who made our lessons really fun, she really thought about how to make it mean something to us and how we could do it in a way that was exciting. We didn't want her to leave.

Nina is a Year 10 pupil:

They need to want to do stuff with us ... sometimes they don't try to manage us and some people will see what they can get away with. They need to be our teacher, we don't like it when they try to be our friend ... we already have friends!

Parent voice

Kathryn comments:

We don't mind our son having student teachers at all if they are able to make sure that he learns what he has to know ... Some student teachers can be good because they are really enthusiastic and do things in a new and exciting way, which our son loves. Some are not so good and then our son loses faith in them, it doesn't seem to take long for him to get fed up with those teachers.

What support can you expect from others?

Whichever pathway into teaching you take there are lots of different people you can go to for help and support. For example, you can draw on support from the school, training providers, your subject professional organisation, teaching unions, other student teachers and, of course, your friends and family.

All parties that are involved with ITE have a vested interest in training good teachers, encouraging good practice in their subject area and providing excellent learning in their schools.

Good classroom practice

Good classroom practice depends and relies on many things being considered and being in place. Some issues are subject specific but some are more generic to all subject areas. We will look at some of these issues in detail.

Ofsted (2012) published a good practice report on outstanding history teaching in which they highlighted the importance of pupils being given opportunities to engage with the '*awe and wonder*' of the subject. They said the lesson was outstanding and that this

> *had been achieved because of the planning of the activities, the opportunities for ongoing reflection, feedback and consolidation, and the clarity of the structure of the lesson. Students knew what they were studying, how they were going to do this and why it was important.*
>
> (Ofsted, 2012, p 5)

This commentary on outstanding practice can be applied equally to all subjects. Experienced teachers tend to say that they can get a 'feel' for what good classroom practice is like. They talk about how the pupils are engaged and engrossed in their work, how they are able to work independently, how they are enthusiastic about the subject and their learning, how they are able to talk about their learning including their strengths and weaknesses and what they need to do to improve. When you consider that there might be 30 different pupils with a variety of different learning needs you may start to appreciate that it takes a great deal of commitment from the teacher to achieve this. Furthermore, good classroom practice is not limited to the lesson content but also includes many more facets such as good organisation, innovative teaching strategies, effective behaviour management, meticulous lesson planning including planning for all pupils to have the opportunity to make progress whatever their ability or learning needs, effective marking of pupils' work showing them how to improve, reporting to parents/carers and others, and of course excellent subject and curriculum knowledge.

Our beliefs about classroom management are that teachers need to be calm, fair and consistent to create a classroom environment that is conducive to teaching and learning. This involves designing a safe, welcoming, stimulating and well-managed classroom where high quality relationships lead to a mutually respectful atmosphere. Classroom management consists of managing and organising the physical space and the available resources, the time, the people, the learning and the pupils' behaviour.

A teacher needs to set explicit high expectations for all pupils, which will inspire, motivate and challenge them. Teachers need to be well organised in their own thinking, planning and behaviour, acting as role models to create a positive and purposeful learning environment. They need to develop key management skills such as effective communication for organising and working with others. Teachers need to establish and follow clear rules and routines for positive behaviour management while addressing any behavioural issues quickly and fairly. It is imperative to have an awareness of school and government policies and to understand what support is available to help you develop good classroom management.

Challenges to good classroom practice

There are many challenges to good classroom practice. Observation of other lessons, classes and pupils in the school and how other teachers deal with specific challenges is beneficial. Good planning and adaptability is key. Taking time after teaching to reflect on what went well and strategies that were successful is also important – it helps to clarify what good classroom practice is and how to develop it in the future.

Some of the considerations you need to be aware of are shown in Table 7.1.

Table 7.1 How to address the challenges of classroom management.

Classroom management issue	How might this be a challenging issue?	Ways to address the issue
Time restraints	Secondary teaching is nearly always organised according to a rigid timetable. Firstly, you have to consider what can realistically be fitted into one lesson (including clearing up) and secondly how a series of lessons over a given period must address the curriculum content.	Observe experienced teachers. Think about how lessons are structured to include the required skills and content within a lesson or sequence of lessons. Schools might have required elements that you need to incorporate in your planning such as setting homework. Be prepared to make adjustments during a lesson; some task might need to be lengthened or shortened.
Limited resources	The school or department might not be able to provide the resources that you want.	Be realistic about your expectations. Be wary about wasting materials. Look at alternative ways of facilitating the same learning with available resources.
Dependence on ICT	Reliance on information and content accessed electronically may be problematic; sometimes the technology might not work.	Do not plan a lesson that is solely dependent on technologies or specific equipment being available. Always have a plan B – consider how you might teach the focus for learning in another way. Be able to justify how the use of your chosen ICT supports learning better than other methods.
Size of groups	Large and small group sizes can provide different challenges in terms of managing resources, ensuring pupils are making progress and that the learning is inclusive.	Use seating plans and consider how you group pupils. Have tasks clearly displayed so all pupils are aware of expectations. Think of ways of recording progress such as photographs or screen shots.
A range of pupil abilities	You may have a wide range of abilities and attitudes to learning within a class (even if they are set by ability). You need to be able to respond to the strengths and needs of all pupils. You have to plan for differentiation so that all pupils can access the learning.	Get to know your pupils and their abilities (find out what data is held by the school and how to use it). Look at ways of making learning accessible for all. Think about different ways of communicating information. Have step-by-step stages prepared; think about using peer support in the classroom. Have additional more challenging activities ready.

Table 7.1 (cont.)

Classroom management issue	How might this be a challenging issue?	Ways to address the issue
Working productively with Learning Support Assistants (LSAs)	There might be a range of different LSAs who may be expected to support a number of different pupils within the class.	Whenever possible make sure that LSAs are aware of the content and learning objectives of the lesson and how they are specifically supporting individuals or groups of pupils. If possible, have communication with LSAs prior to the lesson.
Behaviour	Disruptive behaviour which inhibits pupils' own and possibly others' learning; non-compliance.	Be aware of the school's behaviour policy – know what is acceptable and what is not. Address the behaviour and remain calm and have consistent rules and consequences. Praise good behaviour and use the school's rewards policy. Know what motivates your pupils; be prepared to ask for help and support.
Lack of subject knowledge	There may well be areas of your subject that you are less familiar and confident with and that you have to practise, develop and revise prior to teaching.	If it is a less familiar area you will need to allow extra time in order to carefully plan and practise activities. Look for opportunities to develop your subject knowledge, including seeking out specialists. Ask department staff for ideas. Keep up to date with subject and curriculum information; there is a wealth of teaching material available (good sources are professional subject bodies and associations). Share resources with colleagues.
Understanding the nature and importance of your subject	Some people might consider your subject area to be less important than others in the curriculum. It is important to recognise a subject's own discrete value and how it aids the development of key skills.	You will be an ambassador for your subject area. Have the patience to explain the importance of your subject. Be prepared to offer a strong rationale for the place of your subject in the secondary curriculum.
Special educational needs and disabilities (SEND)	There will be a range of pupils with different needs and abilities in most classes.	Get to know the needs of the pupils and how you might support them. Talk to the SEND specialist.
Clarity of instructions	You might think that your instructions are clear and accessible but the pupils might not think so.	Be prepared to reiterate instructions during the lesson. Think about how you can explain things in different ways. Question the pupils about their understanding of the instructions.

Reflective task

○ Looking at the issues presented in Table 7.1, suggest which ones might pose the greatest challenge for you? Are there any other challenging issues you can think of?

○ Ask some secondary school pupils for their perspectives, or look at your own experience as a learner and consider what a teacher needs to do to make sure that pupils can learn well in lessons.

EFFECTIVE BEHAVIOUR MANAGEMENT

One of the main concerns about working in schools voiced by teachers is that of behaviour management. Disruptive behaviour is a major source of frustration and dissatisfaction for many teachers. In a 2010 survey, 70 per cent of respondents reported that they had considered quitting teaching because of poor behaviour (Teacher Support Network and Family Lives Behaviour Survey, 2010).

Reflective task

○ What do you consider to be disruptive or poor behaviour in a classroom?

○ How do you think you might deal with these behaviours?

○ What support should you expect from your school?

Behaviour management problems are more likely to occur when the teacher has not planned an interesting and engaging lesson that has relevance to the learners. It is also more likely if the pupils are not able to sufficiently engage with the things that help with their learning. If the pupils cannot understand instructions, do not have the skills or confidence to tackle the task, have not got the right materials or resources that they need, they will feel demotivated or unchallenged. Consequently, they will not engage or cannot suitably attempt to engage with learning. You will be encouraged to build positive relationships with your pupils so that you will know them and what they find easy or difficult to do. You will be required to consider the individual learning needs of the pupils when planning a lesson for a class and to be creative in your planning. For some pupils English might not be their first language, some might have poor literacy or numeracy skills or lack self-esteem. Even the most challenging pupils can settle in a lesson and enjoy the experience when the teachers plan with them in mind.

Nonetheless, at times poor and disruptive behaviour can occur and result from factors that may be outside of the class teacher's immediate control. Young people face a multitude of different pressures and expectations that they may bring to school. These can be caused through emotional, social and developmental issues. For example, a pupil may be facing difficulties at home that cause them to present as angry, tired and inconsistent (Delaney, 2010). A pupil might be disengaged or disaffected for a number of reasons and this is why knowing your pupils is vitally important.

On an ITE programme you will be given a great deal of support for developing effective behaviour management and support if things do go wrong – from the school, the ITE provider and your peers. The school will have a clear behaviour management policy that will clarify the expectations of pupils in the classroom and the rewards and sanctions that can be employed.

Reflective task

o Think of an effective secondary classroom teacher that you have encountered. How did they manage behaviour? Did they manage the behaviour so that the lesson could proceed or did they plan the lesson to ensure that the behaviour was manageable?

Teacher voice

How might other people manage behaviour?

Andy: *Having worked in two different schools with different policies I find that if pupils are engaged and the pace is appropriate for the task and their understanding, they become interested and want to learn and participate. I aim to make my lessons engaging. Behaviour becomes less of an issue as the pupils are keen to take part.*

Kirsty: *Mutual respect and empathy are crucial. You have to try to see things from the pupils' point of view while upholding school policies. Sometimes pupils don't like it or feel sanctions can be unfair but in the long run it clarifies the boundaries. When teachers are consistent in their expectations pupils feel secure and know where they stand.*

Julie: *I think that poor behaviour is usually a symptom of poor planning. When you have a very 'difficult' class you need to find out what they are interested in and how they work well. I had a very tricky class that responded well to having short, punchy tasks, competition and sport-related contexts. For example, when teaching about accuracy and precision I took them onto the field to take free kicks. They loved it and were able to understand the science.*

> **Ismael:** *Everybody has challenging classes and behaviour at some point. It is surprising just how draining and demoralising that this can be. You put a lot into planning a lesson and getting resources ready and this can be a huge effort, which feels like a waste of time when the pupils just don't care and won't behave. Obviously you need to reflect on this but it is important that you stand back, take a few deep breaths and let it go. Tomorrow is another day and surprisingly the pupils can and will move on quickly; they rarely hold grudges and nor should you.*

Managing the lesson

The arrangement and layout of the classroom is also the responsibility of the teacher and when it is well managed it can lead to a better learning environment. While you are observing lessons consider how the room is organised and how resources are managed. Is there a seating plan? Do pupils move around in the lesson? Do they have to face a board? Are displays used? Why do you think that the teacher has arranged the class in this way, what impact does it have on the learning?

It is important to consider the value of adding variety, interest and new challenges to lessons. A change in direction or task can reinvigorate learning and reignite interest – both for the pupils and the teacher. It is helpful to plan for a rich variety of activities, which may include collaborative group work, puzzles, matching words and meanings, presentations, drama/role play, music and vivid experiences. Never underestimate the value of powerful open-ended probing and developmental questioning.

LEARNING

Even if good classroom management is taking place, there is no guarantee that effective learning is taking place. You need to ensure you are promoting learning too.

Learning is not always about acquiring a new skill but can be about applying, adapting and using skills, knowledge and techniques. Before you can assess that the desired learning is taking place and students are grasping new concepts, it is imperative that you are clear in your own mind about what you want pupils to learn. Once you are clear about this you can decide how you might assess pupils' progress towards your aims. One of the most obvious ways to check progress is being made is to question pupils regularly throughout a lesson. This should then feed into informing future lessons.

Sometimes it is evident that the lesson is going well and learning is taking place; at this point it is good practice to allow the pupils time to pursue the learning and then reflect upon it. Be confident to stand back and also allow pupils a chance to make mistakes; learning can take different forms. The opportunity to think about your learning (or lack of it) can allow for profound understanding. We do not just learn from experience; we learn from reflecting on experience (Dewey, 1933).

There are times when allowing pupils to struggle can be beneficial to learning. It might allow them the possibility of discovery; a concept might be new to them and become more meaningful if they are allowed the space and time to puzzle over it and work it out either individually, in groups or with additional support.

Keeping up a good pace is conducive to learning. Pupils need to be challenged to move forward while being given the opportunity to practise and revisit skills and ideas. Pupils will learn at different rates and may not always learn sequentially which might not fit in with the timescales that you had initially planned. This is a key point where you have to be flexible and adaptable and allow the learning to flow rather than rigidly following your plan. Alternatively, you may find that pupils grasp concepts far more quickly than you envisaged; again, you need to think on your feet and drive the learning forward, possibly beyond where you had planned to go in that lesson. A pace that is inappropriate is likely to result in pupil disengagement and poor behaviour.

A current drive from government and ITE providers is to require teachers to engage in evidence-informed teaching practice. There has been concern that few teachers in the UK continue to engage with educational research after they gain QTS. This is likely to be a key area of focus for future teachers. You will need to be familiar with educational theory and research, and be able to critically reflect upon it and demonstrate how it is shaping the way you teach.

It is also important for teachers to portray themselves as learners and remember that learning is a collaborative experience in the classroom. Knowledge is always changing, sometimes quite radically and in ways that might cause us to question previously held beliefs. This is the essence of learning and should be celebrated and shared.

If we do not expose our pupils to difficult new concepts and do not challenge them to develop thinking and learning skills, we will not be equipping them for their future lives where these transferable skills will allow them to face an ever-changing world. As Schleicher (2010) suggests:

> Schools have to prepare students for jobs that have not yet been created, technologies that have not yet been invented and problems that we don't know will arise.

Reflective task

o Reflect on a time when you have struggled with a new concept or skill. How empowering was it when you had the light bulb moment of understanding and how long did the learning stay with you as compared to learning off by heart without secure understanding?

Differentiation

There is likely to be a range of pupils with differing abilities, aptitudes and needs within a class. As previously stated, it is important to know the makeup of classes and plan accordingly. *Differentiation* applies to a wide variety of teaching techniques and lesson adaptations that are used to support a diverse group of students, with different learning needs in the same classroom at the same time. In all classrooms teachers need to consider and vary their teaching strategies and use well-designed lessons to engage pupils and their interests while addressing distinct learning needs. The basic idea is that all pupils master essential knowledge, concepts and skills, and teachers use different teaching methods to help pupils meet those expectations.

Remember, in any class with more than one pupil there will always be a range of learning needs, so you must develop expertise in this area. Once you start your ITE course you will receive subject-specific training in how to adapt your teaching for the strengths and needs of all learners.

Assessment and monitoring

Schools use a variety of different data systems to predict what individual pupils may achieve in their future examinations. Teachers need to continually monitor and record how pupils are performing in order to guide them towards their potential, to support their learning and to report progress to parents/carers and other adults. You will need to develop an understanding of the systems in place.

One important responsibility for you is to know how pupils are making progress in order to achieve their potential. Teachers need to make use of a range of different methods of assessing pupils' work. You will be expected to give regular feedback, both orally and through accurate marking. Keeping records of pupils' progress can be done in a number of ways, for example, mark books, tracking sheets, photographs, film documentation, voice recording, samples of work. By being keenly aware of your pupils' capabilities, you will be able to respond early to any changes in the quality of their work, allowing for prompt and focused intervention. It is important to remember that progress is not always linear and that pupils should be allowed to make mistakes and experiment. Methods for monitoring progress and assessment requirements are continually changing. Teachers need to be aware of current policies and accepted practices and be adaptable to new initiatives.

Reflective task

- Where and when in the school day might there be time for pupils to respond to your feedback?

- In what ways might pupils be encouraged to respond to feedback?

Technologies

The rise of information communication technology in schools is unstoppable, and developments in ICT encapsulate broader trends in education. ICT touches every aspect of education ... Schools are using their own websites and intranets to make learning resources available online and at any time of day.

(Cohen et al, 2010, p 59)

Young people are sometimes referred to as *digital natives*, meaning they are generally familiar with the use of the internet from an early age. These young people have grown up in a digital world where technology has, for most, always been a part of their lives. Appealing to their interests and involvement in the use of technology to make learning more accessible and possibly relevant is worthwhile. Many schools now have interactive whiteboards which have great potential to add to the dynamics of real interactive learning. An increasing number of schools are providing pupils with computer tablets for use in class and at home. It is important to remember and plan for the fact that technologies can be unavailable and sometimes incompatible to support all programmes. Schools will have policies to support e-safety. Be able to justify how the use of your chosen ICT supports learning better than other methods. Planning a lesson that is solely dependent on technologies or other certain specific equipment being available is a risk; have a plan B – consider how you might be able to facilitate the learning in another way.

MAINTAINING TEACHER WELL-BEING

With all the demands and complexities expected of teachers on a daily basis it is important to understand how to remain confident and resilient. Remaining positive, in control and able to cope with the many aspects of teaching is desirable for all parties involved – you the teacher, the pupils, other members of staff in your school and your own family. Without maintaining your own well-being you cannot expect to manage a classroom effectively; the two are inextricably linked.

As noted in the Series Editor's introduction to this book, being a teacher and learning to teach has been described as a highly '*emotional labour*' which involves both '*delightful highs and distressing lows*' (Bullough, 2009, p 34).

It has been recognised that teacher well-being promotes teacher effectiveness, teacher retention and school performance (Briner and Dewberry, 2007). With this in mind, how do you keep going and deal with the expectations and realities of being an effective teacher?

Make sure you take a regular reality check – what is going well, what is impacting positively and negatively on your well-being? What are you in a position to develop or change? Be positive about reflections and reactions – avoid purely emotive responses to teaching and take a reflective, balanced view. Remain flexible and understand that learning is a process. Attempt to develop an understanding of different styles and different approaches to teaching while acknowledging recognised good practice. Seek out and be prepared to accept constructive feedback – keep an open mind, even when you may feel uncomfortable. Look for and ask for the support of colleagues and ITE providers. Models of resilience and strategies for maintaining well-being are covered in greater depth in Chapter 9.

Teacher voice

Clementine shares an early career teacher's view:

I would say to a newbie or someone who needed advice – find one good friend that you can trust. It doesn't have to be in your department, but someone who you know will listen without judgement. We deal with hundreds of children so we need positive energy to get them to be positive back. Cut out the moaners, go home when you have stopped being productive, take a break, do some work at home so you aren't anxious about the next day and do something unrelated to school. If you can retain your energies and sense of self you are more ready to manage your classes day by day.

CONCLUSION

This chapter has explored issues of classroom management. Vibrant classrooms are rich and stimulating environments where learning and support take place, new things are discovered and explored, and skills and knowledge are developed. They are challenging places for all participants but are managed and led by the teacher. Both pupils and teachers should feel that they belong in the classroom and have responsibilities towards ensuring that the classroom – in its various forms – is an accessible, inclusive and welcoming place. Good classroom management involves acquiring, adapting, honing and changing many skills – it is an art and worth studying and reflecting upon critically.

☑ Progress checklist

Reflective tasks

In this chapter we have asked you to consider several reflective tasks designed to allow you to think about issues of classroom management. By engaging in these tasks you will have contemplated the following:

○ how you wish to be viewed professionally by others;

○ what different people might expect from you;

○ how you will become proactive;

o   the challenges of classroom management – and how you might respond to them;

o   how you might manage behaviour;

o   maintaining a positive outlook in the classroom;

o   strategies for effective learning.

Next steps

Think about the following questions to help you determine your own position in regard to classroom management.

o   What strengths and skills do you already have that you can apply to effective classroom management?

o   What strengths will you need to develop?

 TAKING IT FURTHER

Cohen, L, Manion, L and Morrison, K (2004) *A Guide to Teaching Practice.* 5th ed. London: RoutledgeFalmer.

Covers important basic skills and issues teachers need to be aware of in the classroom.

Delaney, M (2010) *What Can I Do With The Kid Who ...?* Duffield: Worth Publishing Ltd.

A handbook exploring why pupils may behave the way they do and how a teacher might respond.

Loughran, J (2010) *What Expert Teachers Do: Enhancing Professional Knowledge for Classroom Practice.* New York: Routledge.

This book looks at real classroom examples, showing how crucial principles of teaching and learning are translated to classroom management.

Websites, blogs and twitter feeds

There are many excellent websites, blogs and twitter feeds written by teachers that give a real insight into classroom management issues. A few good starting points are:

Paul Dix: www.pivotaleducation.com (accessed 1 July 2015).

Teacher Toolkit: @TeacherToolkit

Tom Bennett's behaviour management blog:

https://community.tes.co.uk/tom_bennett/b/weblog/default.aspx
(accessed 1 July 2015).

REFERENCES

Briner, R and Dewberry, C (2007) *Staff Well-being is Key to School Success*. London: Worklife Support Ltd / Hamilton House.

Bullough, R V, Jr (2009) Seeking Eudaimonia: The Emotions in Learning to Teach and to Mentor, in Schutz, P and Zembylas, M (eds) *Teacher Emotion Research: The Impact on Teachers' Lives*. New York: Springer, 33–53.

Cohen, L, Manion, L and Morrison, K (2010) *A Guide to Teaching Practice*. London: Routledge.

Delaney, M (2010) *What Can I Do With The Kid Who …?* Duffield: Worth Publishing Ltd.

Dewey, J (1933) *How We Think: A Restatement of the Relation of Reflective Thinking to the Educative Process*. 2nd ed. New York: D. C. Heath and Co.

Mundschenk, N, Milner, C and Nastally, B (2011) Effective Classroom Management: An Air Traffic Control Analogy. *Intervention in School and Clinic*, 47(2): 98–103.

Ofsted (2012) *Outstanding Teaching and Learning in History in 100 minutes – Farlingaye High School*. [online] Available at: www.gov.uk/government/publications/outstanding-teaching-and-learning-in-history-in-100-minutes (accessed 31 July 2015).

Schleicher, A (2010) *The Case for 21st-century Learning*. [online] Available at: www.oecd.org/general/thecasefor21st-centurylearning.htm (accessed 6 July 2015).

Teacher Support Network and Family Lives (2010) *Behaviour Survey*. [online] Available at: https://teachersupport.info/sites/default/files/downloads/Teacher%20Support%20Network%20-%20Behaviour%20practical%20guide%20-%20Colour%20-%20Jun%202013.pdf (accessed 6 July 2015).

Working with young people

Karen Murray-Hall and Mel Norman

INTRODUCTION

Pupil performance and well-being go hand in hand. Pupils can't learn if they don't feel safe or if health problems are allowed to create barriers. And doing well in education is the most effective route for young people out of poverty and disaffection.

(DfES, 2004, p 1)

This chapter focuses on some of the facets of working with young people within the context of the secondary school and some of the wider responsibilities of the role of the teacher. Although both authors have worked as subject specialists in secondary schools, we have found the wider role of working with young people in schools to be an enormously enjoyable part of being a teacher. Whatever comes with the job in terms of government directives, it is the young people, their current and future lives, and supporting them in their journey towards adult life, that is at the heart of the teaching profession. This is a huge responsibility and one that needs careful consideration.

CONTEXT: RESPONSIBILITIES OF TEACHERS

The personal and professional conduct of teachers is an element of the Teachers' Standards (Appendix) and there is an expectation that teachers will demonstrate '*consistently high standards*' in this regard. This encapsulates '*high standards of ethics and behaviour, within and outside school*'. The Teachers' Standards Part Two (Appendix) specifically defines '*the behaviour and attitudes which set the required standard for conduct throughout a teacher's career*' in regard to working with young people.

ACADEMIC AND PASTORAL RESPONSIBILITIES

A tutor is a teacher whose subject is the pupil (her)self.

(Marland and Rogers, 2004, p 19)

As a secondary school teacher you will have a subject specialism and it may be the case that your passion for your subject is the reason you want to become a teacher. However, working in a secondary school in England demands more of you than the academic role of being a specialist subject teacher. You will likely have responsibilities as a form tutor and be part of a pastoral team as well as part of a subject team. The pastoral curriculum encompasses the social and personal support that a school offers the young people in its care and you may be asked to teach PSHE. Specialist teachers will have devised a curriculum for you to follow, but you need to be confident that you can take the responsibility for teaching these areas of the curriculum in a sensitive manner if you are to be successful in the wider context of the secondary school where you will be teaching.

Reflective task

o   What do you think your role would be as part of a pastoral team?

o   What would and wouldn't you be happy to support pupils with?

THE ROLE OF THE FORM TUTOR

The Elton Report into behaviour and discipline in English schools (1989) emphasised the need for a pastoral system in schools, which included the structured use of tutorial time. However, the form tutor structure had been embedded in the English school system for decades before that report was published. Students and colleagues from overseas may not be familiar with the concept of the form tutor and their role within the school. Rosenblatt (2002) describes it as *'an alien concept within many international education systems'* (p 21).

The form tutor role and the pastoral curriculum are ever-changing as different governments make different demands on schools and the teaching profession. If you become a form tutor you will have a number of roles to perform, which we summarise below.

Administration

As a form tutor you will have administrative responsibilities such as:

o   data collection;

o   record keeping;

o   monitoring the academic progress of the pupils in the form group;

o   liaising with other members of the school team and with parents.

Pastoral care

In the eyes of the pupils, however, the pastoral role is probably the most significant aspect of the form tutor's role as the form tutor is 'there for them' at all times. As the form tutor you would have a holistic perception of every pupil in your form group whereas subject tutors only see pupils in terms of how well they progress or behave in that particular subject.

As the form tutor, you are a constant part of a pupil's school life since pupils are likely to have a different teacher every hour or so of the school day. In schools with ten-day timetables, pupils will see some teachers very infrequently. The role of the form tutor is therefore a very important one and is different from your role as a subject tutor, although you may be both a form tutor and a subject tutor to some pupils. You will need to develop a rapport with your tutor group so that it is understood that there is a difference between your role as the subject tutor and your role as the form tutor. There is a similar dilemma if you become involved with extra-curricular activities such as sports, dance or drama, since the relationship between you and the pupils will be different in these circumstances than when you are in the role of a subject teacher. The pastoral line manager is normally a year head or head of house, depending on the structure of the school. Being part of a pastoral team is important in regard to finding out where specialist advice can be found and knowing who to refer young people to for specific support. Most schools are likely to be able to call, for example, on education welfare officers, educational psychologists and social services. As the form tutor you will notice when one of the young people in your care is in need of support. Additionally, the young person is likely to approach you as his/her form tutor when a problem arises, rather than another adult in the school.

Research focus

Jones. J (2011) Beyond the Subject Curriculum: The Form Tutor's Role, in Dillon, J and Maguire, M (eds) *Becoming a Teacher: Issues in Secondary Education.* Maidenhead: Open University Press.

Jane Jones undertook a small research project investigating the role of the form tutor and her findings illustrate some of the diverse demands of the form tutor.

Head, J (2001) Adolescence, in Dillon, J and Maguire, M (eds) *Becoming a Teacher: Issues in Secondary Education.* Maidenhead: Open University Press.

John Head suggests that teenagers have four major concerns which will influence your role as a form tutor:

1. *tensions at home*

2. *school demands encroaching on 'personal time'*

3. *lack of aim in life*

4. *social and sexual relations.*

(Head, 2001, p 140)

Student teacher voice

Student teacher perceptions of the role of the form tutor

Josh: *For me, a form tutor can have a very strong influence on a group of pupils; the first 15 minutes of the day in which the class and form tutor meet before the actual 'school day' begins can really set the tone and mood for the day.*

> *Being available for pupils to talk to sends a very strong message of support, something that a lot of pupils need.*
>
> **Catia:** *In my experience, the form tutor is someone the pupils can talk to in a more open way. I think the pastoral system is good to deal with problems not related to teaching. This is very new to me; where I come from we didn't have anything like this.*
>
> **Anaïs:** *I believe the form tutor role to be the link between pupils and the subject teachers of the pupils. The relationship between a form tutor and his/her pupils is key. The one person the pupils should feel comfortable speaking to is the form tutor.*

Reflective task

o The role of the form tutor is multifaceted. What particular challenges do you think it will pose for you?

o How will you prepare to meet those challenges?

What makes a good form tutor?

Table 8.1 shows the results of our own survey of 38 Year 7 pupils who were asked about the characteristics of a good form tutor.

Table 8.1 What makes a good form tutor?

CHARACTERISTIC	% OF PUPILS
Fun/sense of humour	66%
Kind	58%
Helpful (with problems/organisation)	26%
Being on time	26%
Caring	26%
Being strict at the right times	16%
Being there for you / listening	13%

NB: Other characteristics listed were: being fair; respecting pupils; being happy; being friendly; being honest; not being forgetful.

Jones (2011) concluded from her research investigating the role of the form tutor:

> *It is a role that, though challenging and changing, is immensely rewarding, and a good form tutor, who adheres to being firm, friendly and fair, and funny if possible, is rarely forgotten.*

(Jones, 2011, p 380)

Reflective task

Imagine yourself as a form tutor. What characteristics do you think you could bring to the role? What type of culture would you like to create in your form group? Reflect on how this could best be achieved (think in terms of the physical environment as well as affective factors).

Vertical and horizontal structures for form tutoring

The organisation of the pastoral system varies between schools but many schools tend to be structured along vertical or horizontal lines. The notion of pastoral care and, in particular the house system, germinated in public schools and by the 1970s it had become widely adopted by comprehensive schools (Brooks et al, 2012). Under this type of vertical system, pupils are assigned to a house upon entry to a school and remain in the same house, normally with the same head of house, for their school career. One advantage of the house system is that it facilitates interaction between students from different year groups. However, this system was gradually replaced by a horizontal system and a study conducted by Best (1999) confirmed the overwhelming predominance of horizontal pastoral structures within the maintained sector. The arguments for adopting horizontal grouping, whereby pupils are divided into tutor groups with others from the same year group, tend to be that administrative and developmental issues are likely to be similar when pupils are all at the same stage.

In recent years, however, vertical tutoring has seen something of a resurgence. This could be attributed, at least in part, to the emphasis on personalised learning and pupil voice over the last decade or more. In considering 'deep learning', Hargreaves (2006) states that learning conversations should take place not only between teachers and pupils but also '*between students, and perhaps especially in academic peer tutoring and in mentoring between students of different ages in vertical pastoral systems*' (p 20). Advocates of vertical tutoring claim that it enhances relationships between pupils of different ages, reduces bullying and improves behaviour. It can be empowering for the older pupils in the group, giving them a greater sense of responsibility and developing leadership skills.

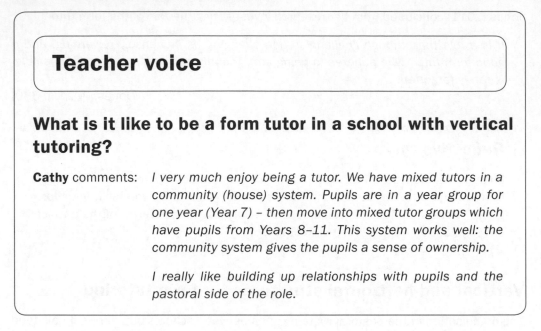

Teacher voice

What is it like to be a form tutor in a school with vertical tutoring?

Cathy comments: *I very much enjoy being a tutor. We have mixed tutors in a community (house) system. Pupils are in a year group for one year (Year 7) – then move into mixed tutor groups which have pupils from Years 8–11. This system works well: the community system gives the pupils a sense of ownership.*

I really like building up relationships with pupils and the pastoral side of the role.

Academic tutoring

As a form tutor, one of your responsibilities would be to monitor your tutees' academic performance. Academic tutoring constitutes an important element of pastoral care today as a form tutor is in a position to be able to monitor their tutees' progress across the entire curriculum and is likely to spot areas where a pupil might be under-performing relative to others. As part of the academic tutoring role the form tutor is typically involved in fostering a learning community, helping pupils talk about their learning, self-assess, set targets and become aware of effective metacognitive strategies (learning how to learn). When communicating with parents it is important that a form tutor can demonstrate a good understanding of their tutees' overall academic attainment and progress as well as their general well-being. This aspect of the form tutor's role bridges the pastoral and the academic systems.

In their review of school time structures over the past 30 years, Symonds and Hagell (2011) found that pupils today are accessing more pastoral care time than before although the time they spend within a school structure has remained more or less consistent over the past three decades. Many schools have witnessed a change in the composition of their workforce and this has had a further impact on the definition of the form tutor's role. For example, in some schools roles that were traditionally the domain of teaching staff are now increasingly undertaken by support staff (learning mentors, cover supervisors, higher level teaching assistants, non-teaching pastoral leads). Edmond and Price (2009) argue that this is particularly the case with regard to the pastoral function in schools and question whether the diversification of roles has contributed to the segmentation of the pastoral and the academic.

As emphasised in the introduction to this chapter, pupil performance and well-being are inextricably linked. Schools are charged with ensuring that pupils' holistic development is taken into account, and in catering for pupils' affective education it becomes clear that any separation between the pastoral and the academic is unhelpful.

> *It is important to note that all curriculum areas impact on pupils' understanding of the world and can influence their developing sense of 'being' and 'belonging'. Whether it is through the choice of curriculum content, the way that learning takes place or the pupils' perceptions of how they are treated, every experience within school plays a part in their developing sense of identity and morality.*
>
> (Brooks et al, 2012, p 332)

Reflective task

Do you see your future career in a pastoral or subject-centred role or both?

SAFEGUARDING

A statutory responsibility

The need for secondary teachers to take a holistic view of pupils' development has already been emphasised and is a requirement of being a teacher in England. The Children Act of 2004 placed a statutory responsibility on schools to engage in multi-agency co-operation to ensure the safeguarding and well-being of children. As a form tutor, you may be the first point of contact for a pupil who is at risk in some way or you may notice that there has been a change in the behaviour of one of the members of your tutor group.

It is a legal requirement (DCSF, 2010) that all schools have a nominated person in charge of safeguarding although the responsibility to provide a safe environment conducive to learning lies with all school staff (DfE, 2014b). Safeguarding, which encompasses child protection issues, can be defined as:

> *protecting children from maltreatment; preventing impairment of children's health or development; ensuring that children grow up in circumstances consistent with the provision of safe and effective care; and taking action to enable all children to have the best outcomes.*
>
> (DfE, 2014b, p 4)

This most recent statutory guidance on safeguarding highlights the need for all staff members to receive appropriate child protection training and to be familiar with safeguarding systems within their school or college.

It is your responsibility to know the school's safeguarding policy and to know what to do when a pupil raises a concern for you. You are not a counsellor and you are not allowed to hold confidences if a pupil gives you sensitive information. Every school has a designated member of the senior management team responsible for the school safeguarding policy and that person will be able to give you appropriate advice and, if seen as the best course of action, can refer a pupil to other agencies for support.

Promoting pupil welfare

A recent research report on safeguarding (Lefevre et al, 2013) identified good practice in those secondary schools where specific child protection needs were addressed along-side pupils' general welfare and where pupils were equipped with the language to voice concerns. Such schools typically had invested time and resources into developing participatory and pupil-centred ways of working.

One such example of good practice is peer mentoring, which has become more widely adopted in secondary schools in recent years. This involves pupils from older year groups (typically Year 9 and above) acting as mentors for younger pupils. Such a system can provide a valuable outlet for younger pupils, enabling them to discuss their concerns on issues such as bullying, family relationships or difficulties with school subjects.

E-safety

The growth in the use of the internet and social media has created difficulties in terms of safeguarding pupils as abuse can go unnoticed if it relates to cyberbullying; during your training you will be given guidelines regarding e-safety. Schools also have policies with regard to the use of the internet and mobile phones during the school day. As a form tutor, you may find yourself the custodian of mobile phones and tablets until the end of the school day, to avoid misuse by pupils during the school day.

Reflective task

Pupils need to understand risk and take some responsibility for their own actions and safety. How can teachers ensure a balance between safeguarding and risk-taking so that pupils are not 'wrapped in cotton wool' during school days?

THE PERSONAL, SOCIAL, HEALTH AND ECONOMIC CURRICULUM

As a form tutor, there is also an expectation that you will contribute to the Personal, Social and Health Education (PSHE) curriculum. PSHE has been part of the national curriculum for secondary schools since 2000. Following the NC review in 2006/07 it became Personal, Social, Health *and Economic* Education. Despite a number of reviews of the subject's place within the curriculum the decision not to make PSHE statutory (ie a compulsory part of the curriculum in all schools) has been upheld.

The non-statutory status of PSHE notwithstanding, the national curriculum for England (DfE, 2014a) makes it clear that:

> *All schools should make provision for personal, social, health, and economic education (PSHE), drawing on good practice. Schools are also free to include other subjects or topics of their choice in planning and designing their own programme of education.*
>
> (DfE, 2014a, p 5)

A school's PSHE curriculum is key in enabling it to fulfil the requirements set out in the NC, particularly those beyond the academic remit:

> *Every state-funded school must offer a curriculum which is balanced and broadly based and which:*
>
> ○ *promotes the spiritual, moral, cultural, mental and physical development of pupils at the school and of society, and*
>
> ○ *prepares pupils at the school for the opportunities, responsibilities and experiences of later life.*
>
> (DfE, 2014a, p 5)

PSHE is most often taught by non-specialists in maintained secondary schools. A factor to consider is that the 'outcomes' of a PSHE lesson (on drugs, for example) are typically not as easy to assess as they would be in your own subject area. This can seem like a daunting prospect.

What makes the PSHE curriculum different?

Brooks et al (2012, p 344) identify four key differences which distinguish the teaching of PSHE from other subjects in the academic curriculum.

1. The content is often the medium (for example, learning to work collaboratively is both the method as well as the purpose).

2. It is particularly learner-dependent, ie the outcomes of a PSHE lesson depend to a certain extent on pupils' personal engagement with the topic and, in many cases, this cannot be as easily assessed as in other subject areas.

3. It is sensitive in nature and therefore careful handling with regard to the exploration of values is often required.

4. It may include topics which are not covered in any other subject in the curriculum and this perhaps places an even greater demand on the PSHE teacher.

There is no national programme of study for PSHE which means schools are not required to follow any prescribed curriculum. Guidance on PSHE issued by the Department for Education (2013) states:

> *Schools should seek to use PSHE education to build, where appropriate, on the statutory content already outlined in the national curriculum, the basic school curriculum and in statutory guidance on: drug education, financial education, sex and relationship education (SRE) and the importance of physical activity and diet for a healthy lifestyle.*

The *PSHE Association* has produced its own programme of study for Key Stages 1–4 (PSHE Association, 2014) which is based around three core themes: Health and Wellbeing; Relationships; Living in the Wider World. Underpinning these are ten evidence-based principles of good practice in PSHE education that apply across Key Stages 1 to 4, which are shown in Table 8.2.

Table 8.2 Ten principles of PSHE education

---

1. Start where children and young people are: find out what they already know, understand, are able to do and are able to say. For maximum impact involve them in the planning of your PSHE education programme.

2. Plan a 'spiral programme' introducing new and more challenging learning, while building on what has gone before, which reflects and meets the personal developmental needs of the children and young people.

3. Take a positive approach which does not attempt to induce shock or guilt but focuses on what children and young people can do to keep themselves and others healthy and safe and to lead happy and fulfilling lives.

4. Offer a wide variety of teaching and learning styles within PSHE education, with an emphasis on interactive learning and the teacher as facilitator.

---

5. Provide information which is realistic and relevant and which reinforces positive social norms.

6. Encourage young people to reflect on their learning and the progress they have made, and to transfer what they have learned to say and to do from one school subject to another, and from school to their lives in the wider community.

7. Recognise that the PSHE education programme is just one part of what a school can do to help a child to develop the knowledge, skills, attitudes and understanding they need to fulfil their potential. Link the PSHE education programme to other whole school approaches, to pastoral support, and provide a setting where the responsible choice becomes the easy choice. Encourage staff, families and the wider community to get involved.

8. Embed PSHE education within other efforts to ensure children and young people have positive relationships with adults, feel valued and where those who are most vulnerable are identified and supported.

9. Provide opportunities for children and young people to make real decisions about their lives, to take part in activities which simulate adult choices and where they can demonstrate their ability to take responsibility for their decisions.

10. Provide a safe and supportive learning environment where children and young people can develop the confidence to ask questions, challenge the information they are offered, draw on their own experience, express their views and opinions and put what they have learned into practice in their own lives.

(Source: PSHE Association 2014)

How is PSHE taught?

Not only the content but also the mode of teaching PSHE varies between schools. The predominant model is through discreet PSHE lessons (DfE, 2011). Other ways that PSHE is embedded in the curriculum include sessions during form time, through other subjects, through enrichment days or other dedicated events.

In the largest study to date of PSHE education in England (DfE, 2011), it was found that PSHE is accorded a significantly lower status in secondary schools compared with their primary counterparts. Furthermore, the main purpose of PSHE in secondary schools was seen as helping pupils deal with life issues as opposed to personal development (Willis et al, 2013). Another significant finding is that none of the secondary schools in the study considered that PSHE underpinned academic performance (Formby and Wolstenholme, 2012). This was even more pronounced in schools in more affluent areas and which perceived themselves as 'higher achieving schools'; in such cases, PSHE education was awarded less time, support and status (DfE, 2011; Formby and Wolstenholme, 2012).

In relation to the teaching of PSHE in England, Ofsted (2013) reports that:

> *Too many teachers lacked expertise in teaching sensitive and controversial issues, which resulted in some topics such as sexuality, mental health and domestic violence being omitted from the curriculum. This was because subject-specific training and support were too often inadequate. In 20% of schools, staff had received little or no training to teach PSHE education.*

Reflective task

○ How would you feel about being asked to teach some of the sensitive issues outlined above? What kind of training do you think you would need to enable you to do so?

○ Do you think that PSHE should be made statutory in secondary schools?

Pupil voice

Pupil voice refers to the way schools enable pupils to have their say in matters relating to the school. This may allow pupils to discuss general aspects of the school community such as arrangements for eating packed lunches or what clothing the pupils want to wear or it may enable them to have a say in the way their learning is implemented.

Two competitions run by national newspapers in 1967 and 2001 asked pupils to write about 'The school that I'd like'. In spite of the 34-year gap, the outcome in both cases indicated that pupils felt powerless within school and that they were '*passive recipients*' of education rather than '*active learners*' (Driscoll 2011, pp 267–8). The 15,000 entries from pupils in the 2001 survey indicated that they do not want something that was designed for a different time. There seems to have been little change to the lived experience of school. Many of the children wrote about the changes they would like to see in schools but expected adults to fail them again (Burke and Grosvenor, 2003 p 152). Our own small survey conducted for this chapter revealed a similar outcome as can be seen in the following *Pupil voice* section below.

Schools that you work in are likely to have developed strategies for addressing pupil voice through a school council or parliament where pupils from each form, year group or house represent the views of their peers and discuss issues with representatives from the teaching staff. Whether the issues discussed are what could be called 'housekeeping' or whether they also include aspects of the curriculum will depend on the individual school. In some schools, pupils are included in the selection and interviewing process when appointing new teachers; feedback from pupils on 'interview lessons' can be a key factor in appointing new staff. What is clear is that Ofsted inspectors are charged with speaking to pupils about a range of aspects relating to their school so there is more pressure on senior managers to ensure that pupils' voices are heard in schools.

Pupil voice

Perceptions of pupil voice in one school

Ella: *The school says they want our opinion but this is often disregarded and they usually end up doing what they want to do. However, some changes have been made in the past influenced by what we want, eg the introduction of a school collegium which is our version of a School Council. There are representatives from every year and they have meetings once every half term. This year they've started being led by the head boy and girl in the lower sixth, with a deputy head supervising.*

Jay: *We would like to have a say in how departments spend their money – at the moment all money goes to PE because it's the favourite department but this means a lot of other departments like music are suffering because we don't have the necessary equipment.*

Martha: *We also think there should be more interactive learning and we should be able to use our phones in lessons. We would like to be able to talk to teachers about the ways they teach and if we are given punishments like a detention, we would like the opportunity to explain our side of things.*

Research focus

Engaging with pupil voice

Rudduck, J and Flutter, J (2004) *How to Improve your School: Giving Pupils a Voice.* London: Continuum.

The work of Rudduck and Flutter gives a more positive perspective than the account provided above on the way schools engage with pupil voice, indicating a lot of progress but in a relatively small number of schools at the time of the publication of their book. They contend that school structures and patterns of relationships have to be reviewed to enable a school to progress from a learning organisation to a learning community and to begin to embrace pupil voice.

Reflective task

When you were at school were you given the opportunity to engage with decisions about general school practices, for example, uniform or issues related to subject lessons? If yes, did you feel empowered or ambivalent about the process? If no, would you have liked to have been consulted?

CONCLUSION

It is possible that you are thinking of a career in secondary teaching because you have a passion for a particular subject and you are keen to pass on your passion to young people so that they too can engage with a subject you find fascinating and exciting. This chapter has outlined the wider perspectives of working with young people. You will certainly have a subject specialist role in a secondary school but there are obligations upon you to be involved with the holistic development of every pupil you teach. As a form tutor you have a big responsibility for the well-being of the young people in your tutor group, which involves monitoring academic progress as well as the pastoral care of each pupil.

You should embrace the wider role of working with young people, which will enhance your work as a subject specialist and, to quote Jeanette, a head of Year 11:

A pastoral role is one of the most rewarding that a teacher can take on.

 Progress checklist

Reflective tasks

The tasks in this chapter should have helped you to reflect on the qualities needed to be a good form tutor. Are you all those things? Will you be a form tutor who is appreciated by the pupils in the form? If you are required to take on some or all aspects of the PSHE curriculum, will you feel able and prepared for this role?

Next steps

You could seek out additional training for involvement in aspects of the PSHE curriculum; there may be online support which could be helpful in dealing with issues such as cyberbullying and drugs.

▶▶ **TAKING IT FURTHER**

ProTeachersVideo Archive of Safeguarding Guidance for Teachers. [online] Available at: www.proteachersvideo.com/ProgrammeListByVocabularyAnd TermData/69/whole-school-issues/3041/safeguarding-children/ Secondary (accessed 20 February 2015).

Provides helpful advice on safeguarding responsibilities and practice.

Battersby, J and Gordon, J (2006) *Preparing to Teach: Learning from Experience*. Abingdon: Routledge.

Chapter 7 'Learning from the hidden curriculum' gives further insight into being a form tutor, being a role model and PSHE.

Hastings, S (2006) *The Complete Classroom: Issues and Solutions for Teachers*. Abingdon: Routledge.

Contains chapters on personalised learning, pupil power and 22 other classroom 'issues'. The book offers 'a series of stepping stones towards a supportive and inspiring classroom'.

White, J (2011) *Exploring Well-being in Schools*. Abingdon: Routledge.

This book is aimed at teachers, parents and other educators and aims to provide an 'accessible' guide to the issues surrounding the well-being of children in schools.

Blogs and twitter feeds

The following may support your ongoing research into the matters discussed in this chapter.

Childnet (international e-safety organisation): www.childnet.com/blog

PSHE Association: @PSHEassociation

The Relational Schools Project: @RSchoolsProject

REFERENCES

Best, R (1999) The Impact of a Decade of Educational Change on Pastoral Care and PSE: A Survey of Teacher Perceptions. *Pastoral Care in Education: An International Journal of Personal, Social and Emotional Development*, 17(2): 3–13.

Brooks, V, Abbott, I and Huddleston, P (2012) *Preparing to Teach in Secondary Schools: A Student Teacher's Guide to Professional Issues in Secondary Education. 3rd ed.* Maidenhead: Open University Press.

Burke, C and Grosvenor, I (2003) *The School I'd Like*. London: RoutledgeFalmer.

Department for Children, Schools and Families (DCSF) (2010) *Working Together to Safeguard Children: A Guide to Inter-agency Working to Safeguard and Promote the Welfare of Children*. Nottingham: Department for Children, Schools and Families. [online] Available at: www.education.gov.uk/publications/standard/publicationdetail/page1/DCSF-00305-2010 (accessed 20 February 2015).

Department for Education (DfE) (2011) *Personal, Social, Health and Economic (PSHE) Education: A Mapping Study of the Prevalent Models of Delivery and their Effectiveness*. [online] Available at: www.gov.uk/government/uploads/system/uploads/attachment_data/file/219615/DFE-RR080.pdf (accessed 31 July 2015).

Department for Education (DfE) (2013) *Personal, Social, Health and Economic Education*. [online] Available at: www.gov.uk/government/publications/personal-social-health-and-economic-education-pshe/personal-social-health-and-economic-pshe-education (accessed 20 February 2015).

Department for Education (DfE) (2014a) *The National Curriculum in England Key Stages 3 and 4 Framework Document*. Reference: DFE-00183-2013. [online] Available at: www.gov.uk/government/publications/national-curriculum-in-england-secondary-curriculum (accessed 31 July 2015).

Department for Education (DfE) (2014b) *Keeping Children Safe in Education: Statutory Guidance for Schools and Colleges*. Reference DFE-00341-2014. [online] Available at: www.gov.uk/government/uploads/system/uploads/attachment_data/file/372753/Keeping_children_safe_in_Education.pdf (accessed 20 February 2015).

Department for Education and Skills (DfES) (2004) *Every Child Matters: Change for Children in Schools*. Nottingham: Department for Education and Skills. Reference: DfES/1089/2004. [online] Available at: http://dera.ioe.ac.uk/7670/1/DFES-1089-200MIG748.pdf (accessed 23 February 2015).

Driscoll, J (2011) Children's Views on School and Schooling, in Dillon, J and Maguire, M (eds) *Becoming a Teacher: Issues in Secondary Education*. Maidenhead: Open University Press.

Edmond, N and Price, M (2009) Workforce Re-modelling and Pastoral Care in Schools: A Diversification of Roles or a De-professionalisation of Functions? *Pastoral Care in Education: An International Journal of Personal, Social and Emotional Development*, 27(4): 301–11.

Elton Report (1989). *Enquiry into Discipline in Schools*. London: Her Majesty's Stationery Office [online] Available at: www.educationengland.org.uk/documents/elton/elton1989.html#00a (accessed 31 July 2015).

Formby, E and Wolstenholme, C (2012) If There's Going to be a Subject that You Don't Have to Do ...: Findings from a Mapping study of PSHE Education in English Secondary Schools. *Pastoral Care in Education*, 30(1): 5–18.

Hargreaves, D (2006) *A New Shape for Schooling?* London: Specialist Schools and Academies Trust. [online] Available at: www.my-ecoach.com/online/ resources/13729/a_new_shape_for_schooling_11.pdf (accessed 22 February 2015).

Head, J (2001) Adolescence, in Dillon, J and Maguire, M (eds) *Becoming a Teacher: Issues in Secondary Education*. Maidenhead: Open University Press.

Jones, J (2011) Beyond the Subject Curriculum: The Form Tutor's Role, in Dillon, J and Maguire, M (eds) *Becoming a Teacher: Issues in Secondary Education*. Maidenhead: Open University Press.

Lefevre, M, Burr, R, Boddy, J and Rosenthal, R (2013) *Good Practice in Safeguarding and Child Protection in Secondary Schools*. London: Office of the Children's Commissioner. [online] Available at: www.childrenscommissioner.gov.uk/content/ publications/content_710 (accessed 20 February 2015).

Marland, M and Rogers, R (2004) *How to be a Successful Form Tutor*. London: Continuum.

Ofsted (2013) *Not Yet Good Enough: Personal, Social, Health and Economic Education in Schools*. [online] Available at: www.ofsted.gov.uk/resources/130065. (accessed 31 July 2015).

PSHE Association (2014) *Ten Principles of Good PSHE Education*. [online] Available at: www.pshe-association.org.uk/content.aspx?CategoryID=1156 (accessed 31 July 2015).

Rosenblatt, M (2002) Effective Tutoring and School Improvement. *Pastoral Care in Education: An International Journal of Personal, Social and Emotional Development*, 20(4): 21–6.

Rudduck, J and Flutter, J (2004) *How to Improve your School: Giving Pupils a Voice*. London: Continuum.

Symonds, J E and Hagell, A (2011) Adolescents and the Organisation of their School Time: A Review of Changes over Recent Decades in England. *Educational Review*, 63(3): 291–312.

Willis, B, Clague, L and Coldwell, M (2013) Effective PSHE Education: Values, Purposes and Future Directions. *Pastoral Care in Education: An International Journal of Personal, Social and Emotional Development*, 31(2): 99–111.

9 Thriving as a secondary teacher

Nickey Brown and Mark Boylan

INTRODUCTION

The best teachers do not just survive the demands of teaching, they thrive. They are teachers who know why they are doing the job, develop their own teaching style, have good relationships with pupils and colleagues, and have resilience. The aim of this chapter is to help you to prepare to thrive as a secondary teacher by guiding you to:

○ reflect on the personal qualities that make a great secondary teacher, including those that may not be obvious;

○ identify where you feel that you have 'strengths' and which personal attributes you feel you need to develop;

○ consider different styles of teaching and learning as a step to developing your personal style;

○ explore the importance of emotional intelligence in being a teacher;

○ examine the importance of professional resilience, identifying challenges you are likely to face during ITE and your early career;

○ identify practical steps to take to develop your ability to thrive as an inspirational secondary school teacher.

THE IMPORTANCE OF PURPOSE

In Chapter 2, you were encouraged to think about the different reasons that might motivate you to become a secondary teacher. Developing and nurturing a sense of purpose as a teacher is important if you are going to flourish in the profession. Being clear about what you are trying to achieve as a teacher is the foundation on which your success can be built. It can support you through challenging times.

Motivation to be a teacher is personal and different for each teacher. Pay and conditions are important – not least because they signal that society values what teachers do. But teachers who thrive have a wider sense of purpose. Often beginning teachers talk about social responsibility or wanting to make a difference to the lives of young people. For others the motivator is a passion for their subject. Perhaps you have ideas about how schools and the curriculum should be changed. As an individual teacher, particularly one who is just starting out, you may think you cannot have much effect on the teaching profession as whole. However, there are ways in which, individually and collectively, teachers can seek to bring about change in education. Judith Sachs (2003) puts forward the idea of the *activist professional* – this is a teacher who not only seeks to do a good job for the pupils they teach but who works with other teachers to change education in ways they think are important.

Even if you wanted to, schools are not places where it is possible to coast along doing just enough to get by. Quite rightly school leaders, colleagues, parents and, most importantly, pupils, need teachers to be the best teacher they can be, so that must be part of every secondary teacher's sense of purpose.

In our view, great teachers are not born, they develop. Recent international research has also recognised the importance of investing in the development of teachers' professional capital for successful schools (Hargreaves and Fullan, 2012).

Reflective task

In Chapter 2, you were invited to make notes on why you wanted to teach. Look back at your notes and consider your reasons again. Have these changed or developed as a result of reading this book?

You are likely to have many reasons for wanting to teach. One way of reflecting on purpose is through a framework of thinking separately about the purpose for self, others and the wider community and society.

Use the sentences below as starting points for paragraphs of about 50 words that summarise these different purposes.

○ Being a teacher will help me to personally develop by ...

○ Being a teacher will allow me to make a difference to the lives of pupils I teach by ...

○ Being a teacher will support me to make a contribution to society by ...

METAPHORS FOR TEACHING AND LEARNING

In this section we consider metaphors as a tool for thinking about teaching and learning. When you use a different image for a teacher you may, firstly, come to understand more about the role of the teacher and secondly, more about your own views of what teaching is. A metaphor – 'a teacher is a ...' – or its cousin, a simile – 'a teacher is like a ...' can help you to think about something in a new way.

Metaphors for teaching

Metaphors are powerful. As a teacher you will use metaphors to help explain ideas to pupils. They are also useful when reflecting on teaching challenges. For example, a difficult to manage Friday afternoon lesson can feel different when you shift from thinking about the pupils as 'badly behaved' and start to think about them as 'enthusiastic puppies who want to play'. It may lead you to work with the enthusiasm of the pupils rather than battling against it.

During your ITE it's important to learn from others, listen to the advice of more experienced colleagues and try out different successful teaching approaches that you see. That said, a thriving teacher does not simply teach in the way they have learned from others; the best schools expect their experienced teachers to be innovative and to create their own style. One way to do this is by thinking about metaphors for teaching.

Here is a list of common metaphors for being a teacher.

A teacher is …

o   … a news broadcaster

o   … a doctor

o   … a gardener

o   … a sports coach

o   … a mountain guide

o   … an actor

Each of these metaphors suggests different relationships between the teacher and learner, different goals or purposes of teaching and different ideas of how learning happens and what it is to learn.

Here is a summary of an extended metaphor written by a teacher:

> *A teacher is a bandleader, pupils are band members, the objective is the parade. I want to get to know each individual's strengths. From there I would organise them and begin our practices. I would let them 'jam' frequently to learn from each other and see the potential in their peers. I help them to see the importance of the part they play in our band and that the music we produce is just dissonant sounds if we are unable to harmonise.*
>
> (Patchen and Crawford, 2011, p 286)

Reflective task

o   Consider and reflect on the list of metaphors for teaching listed above. In what ways do each of these apply to teaching? Even if you are not drawn to or do not agree with a particular metaphor, see if you can find a way that it might apply to teaching, perhaps with a particular group of learners. What do you learn from this?

o   Choose one or two metaphors and consider what the corresponding metaphor would be for pupils and the aims of teaching. For example, the metaphor 'a teacher is a gardener' implies that pupils are the plants in the garden and the aim of teaching is to grow healthy plants.

Metaphors for learning

The metaphors for teaching also imply metaphors for learning and how it happens. Four metaphors will be introduced here; the first two are long-recognised metaphors for learning – 'learning as acquisition' and 'learning as participation' (Sfard, 1998).

1. *Learning as acquisition* emphasises the idea of knowledge as something that the learner is either given or takes. This metaphor fits well with the learning of facts.

2. *Learning as participation* emphasises the idea of knowing how to act in complex social situations and implies learning by doing alongside others. This metaphor is relevant when applying facts to solve a problem within a group or when participating in a conversation in another language.

Both metaphors are useful and important. The extent to which learning is best seen as acquisition or as participation depends on what is being learned, who is learning, how they are learning and how the teacher is teaching.

More recently, writers have put forward two other metaphors for learning – 'learning as communication' and 'learning as creation'.

3. *Learning as communication* emphasises the two-way process of dialogue between the teacher and pupil and pupils with each other (Sfard, 2008).

4. *Learning as creation* points to the way in which the act of making something or doing something in a new way can represent learning (Paavola, Lipponen and Hakkarainen, 2004). The metaphor is clearly important in school subjects such as art or in the creative aspects of English, drama or music but all subjects involve creativity and learning as creation, even if they are not always thought of in that way. When a pupil develops a formula to describe a pattern in mathematics or designs an experiment in science they may be learning through creation.

These four metaphors provide a map of different approaches to teaching and learning. They can overlap with each other and are interrelated, as is shown in the diagram below.

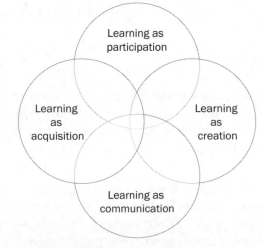

Figure 9.1 Four metaphors for learning

The way teachers blend such approaches together is part of the development of their personal distinctive teaching style. For example, learning computing involves acquiring the syntax of a programming language as well as developing creative problem-solving skills; a teacher will use different approaches to support these two types of learning. You might find some of the metaphors for learning and associated ways of teaching will be more comfortable for you than others. Some will fit better with particular subjects. But a hallmark of successful teachers is that they are adept at all these different approaches and flexibly draw on these different ways of teaching and learning to meet the needs of their pupils.

Reflective task

○   You may have already decided which subject you want to teach; it may be that you're still deciding. Think about the subject or subjects that you are interested in and your own personal approach to learning. How do you want learners in your classroom to learn?

○   Consider the different metaphors for teaching you reflected on earlier. How might these map onto the four metaphors for learning?

Research focus

Extended metaphors for teaching

Patchen, T and Crawford, T (2011). From Gardeners to Tour Guides: The Epistemological Structure Revealed in Teacher-generated Metaphors of Teaching. *The Journal of Teacher Education*, 62(3): 286–98.

This article reports on an analysis of 32 teachers' extended metaphors for teaching. The researchers report that metaphors can broadly be grouped into two types: acquisition and participative. When they shared the results with teachers and further developed the research, they found that teachers often expressed a preference for teaching approaches that were more orientated to pupil participation but their metaphors still tended to focus on acquisition.

WHAT MAKES A GOOD SECONDARY TEACHER?

In this section we invite you to think about the skills and attributes that support your vision of teaching. Some of what follows will be familiar from previous chapters. Here we revisit this in relation to what supports secondary teachers to thrive.

Reflective task

A question that you can anticipate being asked at interview is 'what makes a great secondary teacher?'

○ Think about teachers who inspired you in your own secondary education and those whom you may have observed recently in school. What were the qualities that helped them to teach so well? Think beyond the attributes that they demonstrated while in the classroom to those that it's evident they employ during their preparation, follow up and general administration.

○ Think about the teachers whom you found to be less effective. What were the qualities that they lacked or that were less well developed?

○ Make a list of the skills and attributes that you feel make a great secondary teacher.

Student teacher voice

Below is a list of attributes that our current student teachers feel describe a great teacher. How closely does this list align with the list that you made?

○ *approachable*

○ *communicates well*

○ *consistent and fair*

○ *continuously develops professionally*

○ *creative*

○ *enthusiastic*

○ *establishes clear routines and boundaries*

○ *has a sense of humour*

○ *has strong subject knowledge*

○ *interested in young people*

○ *organised*

○ *patient*

○ *resilient*

Reflective task

○ You are invited to reflect on your personal priorities for development as a teacher. Firstly, look again at the list of skills and attributes of a great secondary teacher that you wrote in response to the reflective tasks above.

○ Select what you think are the most important nine skills, attributes or dispositions from the list.

○ Write each on a piece of paper or card and arrange them in a diamond nine, with the most important at the apex of the diamond, the two next in importance below that and so on until your nine cards are in a diamond shape.

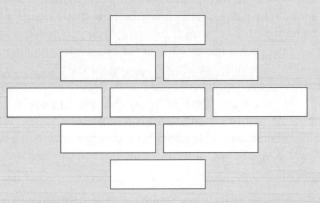

○ How confident do you feel about your strength in each of the attributes? Write a number between 1 and 3 on each card: 1 – this is an area of strength, already well developed; 3 – this is an area that you know needs developing; give a score of 2 to attributes that lie between these two points.

○ Now choose from these attributes those that are priorities for you to develop; this may be because you've scored them 3 or it may be because you've placed them at the top of your diamond. You now should have identified a small number of priorities for development. For each of these consider steps you can take before beginning ITE and during ITE to develop these. In the rest of this chapter we make suggestions for developing many important attributes.

TEACHING WITH EMOTIONAL INTELLIGENCE

Several of your chosen priorities may relate to your emotional intelligence and your ability to build strong relationships with young people. In this section we highlight key aspects of emotional intelligence in teaching and suggest ways that you can develop these.

Emotional intelligence

The idea of emotional intelligence was popularised by Daniel Goleman in his 1995 book *Emotional Intelligence: Why It Can Matter More Than IQ*.

The idea of emotional intelligence is not unproblematic because there is a lot of baggage attached to the word intelligence. It is often thought about as something that is fixed and unchanging but more recently people have questioned that idea. When it comes to the different dispositions that make up emotional intelligence they are all qualities that we can and do develop as teachers.

Why emotional intelligence is important in teaching

The relationships that you build with pupils and with colleagues, and the way in which you talk to them about your subject, will influence how they engage with you and the work that you are doing together. Whatever teaching style you develop, to be successful your relationships with pupils will be key. One of the most challenging aspects of teaching is that it puts you in constant contact with young people; for much of your day you may be working alone with each group that you teach. Recent advances in neuroscience (and evidence from our own experience) show us that young people are still developing and so experimenting with their emotional intelligence, and you will frequently be required to set the emotional tone. This quote from teacher and child psychologist Haim Guinott (1972) made this point about our responsibilities in the classroom 40 years ago and it still rings true today:

> I've come to a frightening conclusion that I am the decisive element in the class-room. It's my personal approach that creates the climate. It's my daily mood that makes the weather. As a teacher, I possess a tremendous power to make a child's life miserable or joyous. I can be a tool of torture or an instrument of inspiration. I can humiliate or heal. In all situations, it is my response that decides whether a crisis will be escalated or de-escalated and a child humanized or dehumanized.
>
> (Guinott, 1972, p 12)

There is another aspect to emotional intelligence and teaching; not only can it help you to foster an emotional state in pupils that is conducive to learning and *their* well-being but it can help *you* to be happy and to thrive in a high pressured environment – and to create an emotional state that is conducive to teaching.

Reflective task

○ Think about the emotional intelligence that supports a great teacher. What are the attributes that effective teachers demonstrate that enable them to work effectively with their colleagues and with young people?

Developing emotional intelligence

How many of the following did you consider?

o empathising – recognising and considering how others feel and developing the ability to respond appropriately;

o knowing how to develop and maintain appropriate relationships with colleagues and pupils, including with those to whom you may not initially (or ever) warm to;

o believing that all people have value and that all pupils can progress.

o being committed to being open and honest – a willingness to admit when you've made a mistake or acted in haste;

o being able to recognise and manage your own emotions, for example, being able to control your anger;

o being willing to ask for help when necessary.

Being a great secondary teacher is a tall order! It's important to realise that no teacher has all of these skills; great teachers are constantly working to maximise their strengths and to develop from their weaknesses.

You will **strengthen** your emotional intelligence through teaching but you can start to develop your awareness of important issues by observing experienced teachers.

Reflective task

Use the checklist below to reflect on the lessons you have observed.

o Was the language that was used to speak to pupils inclusive and positive?

o How did the teacher use eye contact to engage pupils?

o Was the teacher alert to non-verbal communication (pupil posture, eye contact, facial expressions, pace of movement) and how did they demonstrate their response to it?

o What impact did the teacher's non-verbal communication have (movement around the room, tone of voice, facial expression, posture)?

o How did the teacher use pupils' names?

o How did the teaching and learning activities help the teacher to get to know their pupils as individuals?

o What did the teacher do to anticipate the hopes or concerns of their pupils? These may include 'Will I have to speak?', 'Will this be relevant to me?', 'How will I be tested?'.

o Was there genuine dialogue and if so, how did the teacher facilitate this?

As a beginning teacher you will need to translate your personal goals into specific targets for each lesson to develop your ability to successfully interact with pupils and to demonstrate your emotional intelligence to others.

RESILIENCE

Resilience has recently become something of a buzz word and the capacity to demonstrate resilience is now considered as part of admissions to ITE. The term resilience was first used extensively in relation to children's capacity to deal with challenges when growing up under adverse circumstances. Since then interest has grown in the resilience of particular groups of people and in different contexts. Teacher resilience is a particular form of professional resilience which enables teachers to stay in the profession and stay professional. If resilience means simply keeping on doing the job, then that is surviving rather than thriving.

Various definitions of teacher resilience have been proposed by researchers and others:

○ *a quality that enables teachers to maintain their commitment to teaching and their teaching practices despite challenging conditions and recurring setbacks.*

(Brunetti, 2006, p 813)

○ *a capacity to continue to 'bounce back', to recover strength or spirit quickly in the face of adversity ... a dynamic construct subject to influence by environmental, work specific and personal contexts.*

(Sammons et al, 2007, p 694)

○ *the capacity to overcome personal vulnerabilities and environmental stressors, to be able to 'bounce back' in the face of potential risks and to maintain well-being.*

(Oswald et al, 2003, p 50)

Research focus

Early career resilience

Probst, H, Boylan, M, Nelson, P and Martin, R (2014) Early Career Resilience: Interdisciplinary Insights to Support Professional Education of Radiation Therapists. *Journal of Medical Imaging and Radiation Sciences*, 45(4): 390–8.

A recent study of the resilience of early career professionals in different professions, including teaching participants, pointed to the dual nature of resilience. While the ability to bounce back was important, what the student teachers and early career teachers described as more important was dealing with the ongoing day-to-day challenge of working in a demanding role. Resilience is not just about coping under particular strains but about coping every day.

The challenges of beginning teaching

In Chapter 2, five issues were identified as important challenges for teachers: workload; work-life balance; stress / exhaustion; pupil behaviour and discipline; pressure of government policies and change (for example, Ofsted).

When you are beginning teaching there is another important challenge that should not be underestimated. Entering into a new work environment is stressful and challenging, whether as a student teacher or as an NQT. Relationships with colleagues, including your school mentor, are important sources of support.

Many student teachers are fortunate to have supportive and experienced mentors who help them to develop, although that is not always the case (Hobson and Malderez, 2013). Here is an account from one beginning teacher about her placement experience.

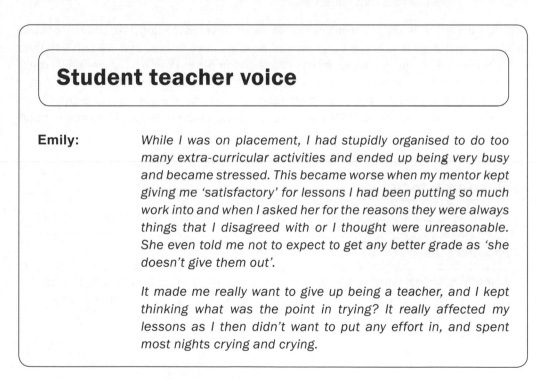

Student teacher voice

Emily: *While I was on placement, I had stupidly organised to do too many extra-curricular activities and ended up being very busy and became stressed. This became worse when my mentor kept giving me 'satisfactory' for lessons I had been putting so much work into and when I asked her for the reasons they were always things that I disagreed with or I thought were unreasonable. She even told me not to expect to get any better grade as 'she doesn't give them out'.*

It made me really want to give up being a teacher, and I kept thinking what was the point in trying? It really affected my lessons as I then didn't want to put any effort in, and spent most nights crying and crying.

Emily was able to overcome these challenges by drawing on her personal qualities and the support of her personal networks and other teachers in the school. When applying for her first post, she looked for schools which would support her to develop as a teacher. At interview it is a good idea to ask questions about the programme of support for NQTs. Fortunately, Emily's story is different from the experience of the majority of beginning teachers but it is still important to have a good personal support network to draw on when faced with challenges in school.

A positive outlook

One way to support resilience is to develop a positive outlook. An approach to this developed by Martin Seligman is the idea of learned optimism (Seligman, 2011). At its root this involves 'unlearning' ways of thinking about the world and ourselves which undermine us and learning alternatives which help us move forward and succeed. Learned optimism does not mean pretending everything is okay when it is not; it is about how we respond to the situations that life brings.

Learned optimism is part of what is known as positive psychology. Another aspect of positive psychology is to focus on gratitude. Studies have shown that we can enhance our sense of well-being, lower our stress levels and improve our physical health by regularly remembering to reflect on experiences or aspects of our lives that we are grateful for. Even when teaching brings challenges, one way to see the bigger picture is to cultivate a sense of gratitude that you have the opportunity to do such interesting and worthwhile work.

Research focus

Mansfield, C, Beltman, S, Price, A and McConney, A (2012) Don't Sweat the Small Stuff: Understanding Teacher Resilience at the Chalkface. *Teaching and Teacher Education*, 28(3): 357–67.

Something we have found that supports beginning teachers' resilience is to use a model of resilience to talk about it. The diagram in Figure 9.2 was developed from a study of 200 graduating and early career teachers and proposes four dimensions.

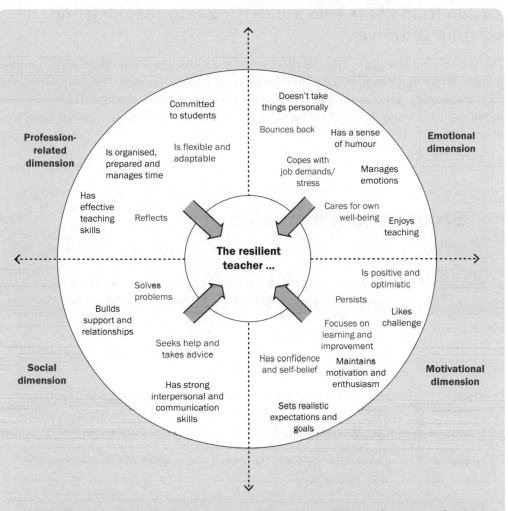

Fig 9.2 A four-dimensional framework of teacher resilience, from Mansfield
et al, 2012, p 362, reproduced by kind permission of Elsevier Limited

This diagram points to the multifaceted nature of resilience. This suggests
that there is not one way to be resilient. It is also important to be aware that in
resilience some qualities can be 'double edged' – they can cut two ways. For
example, throughout this book, authors have emphasised the importance of a
sense of purpose and professionalism. Yet being overcommitted to the job has
its own pitfalls such as finding it difficult to unwind, or spending too much time on
preparation and so arriving tired to the classroom. Similarly, empathy is important
but so is the ability to 'detach' from an issue so that you can effectively offer your
professional support to pupils.

What is more important than trying to find a recipe for resilience is to develop
the self-awareness to know your strengths and also the areas that are more
challenging for you. To frame this positively we might call these our learning
edges.

Advice from those who are getting into teaching and starting to thrive

Those who are currently in ITE and succeeding have important advice on what you need to do to thrive as a secondary teacher. We asked a group of student teachers with whom we are currently working about what makes a great secondary teacher. They were keen to highlight the importance of taking care of yourself during your ITE. Below is some of their advice.

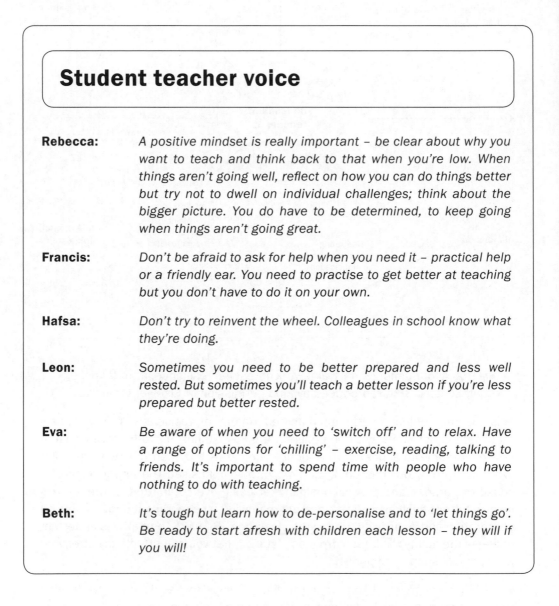

Student teacher voice

Rebecca: *A positive mindset is really important – be clear about why you want to teach and think back to that when you're low. When things aren't going well, reflect on how you can do things better but try not to dwell on individual challenges; think about the bigger picture. You do have to be determined, to keep going when things aren't going great.*

Francis: *Don't be afraid to ask for help when you need it – practical help or a friendly ear. You need to practise to get better at teaching but you don't have to do it on your own.*

Hafsa: *Don't try to reinvent the wheel. Colleagues in school know what they're doing.*

Leon: *Sometimes you need to be better prepared and less well rested. But sometimes you'll teach a better lesson if you're less prepared but better rested.*

Eva: *Be aware of when you need to 'switch off' and to relax. Have a range of options for 'chilling' – exercise, reading, talking to friends. It's important to spend time with people who have nothing to do with teaching.*

Beth: *It's tough but learn how to de-personalise and to 'let things go'. Be ready to start afresh with children each lesson – they will if you will!*

Research focus

Managing your cortisol: the importance of embodiment

White, J and Gardner, J (2012) *The Classroom X-Factor: The Power of Body Language and Nonverbal Communication in Teaching.* Abingdon: Routledge.

It is now well established that the way that we 'self-talk', how we think about ourselves and our experiences, can affect our resilience and our stress levels. It is also well established that body language is important to communication and how we are seen by others and see others. White and Gardner relate how research has underlined that body posture can have a direct and immediate effect on the key stress hormone cortisol and the key status hormone testosterone – which is linked to our sense of self-esteem and confidence.

Cuddy, A (2012) Your Body Language Shapes Who You Are. *TEDGlobal.* [online] Available at: www.ted.com/talks/amy_cuddy_your_body_language_shapes_who_ you_are?language=en (accessed 30 July 2015).

In this TED talk social psychologist Amy Cuddy shares her research showing that by adopting open postures – what she calls power poses – for just a few minutes, we can reduce our stress and increase our sense of self-confidence. Importantly for teachers, this is picked up by others and you are therefore more likely to be treated with respect or seen as capable. In the study, she found that people who spent a few minutes managing their cortisol levels before going into an interview were more likely to be employed.

CONCLUSION

This chapter has aimed to help you to reflect on what is needed to thrive as a secondary teacher. It has considered a range of issues that are important now, as you consider applying to teach, and which will also be important during your career. Some of the factors that we have identified as key to thriving are being clear about your purpose as a teacher, developing your own teaching style, strengthening your emotional intelligence and being aware of the importance of resilience.

 Progress checklist

Reflective tasks

By engaging in the reflective activities in the chapter you have:

○ considered what your purposes as a teacher might be;

○ started to develop your own metaphor for being a teacher;

○ reflected on the qualities of a successful teacher and on which areas are priorities for you to develop;

○ considered a lesson you have observed in school and identified ways in which emotional intelligence is important to successful teachers;

○ begun to identify ways to support your resilience as a teacher.

Next steps

○ Use the reflective tasks and notes you have made from this chapter to help you to write your ITE application and to prepare for interviews.

○ There is much written on teaching styles, emotional intelligence and teacher resilience. Follow up some of the sources we have pointed to in this chapter.

▶▶ **TAKING IT FURTHER**

Allen, V (2014) *Understanding and Supporting Behaviour through Emotional Intelligence*. Northwich: Critical Publishing.

This book looks at the relationship between teachers' emotional intelligence and pupil behaviour. It combines both theory and practice, encourages reflection and offers lots of ideas and resources.

Joyce, B, Calhoun, E and Hopkins, D (2009). *Models of Learning: Tools for Teaching*. Buckingham: Open University Press.

If you are interested in reading more about models of learning and the implications for teaching, then this book is valuable and Chapter 12 is particularly relevant.

Blogs and twitter feeds

Ken Robinson, Changing Paradigms, *RSA Animates*. [online] Available at: www.youtube.com/watch?v=Z1ylOMFYzXc (accessed 31 July 2015).

Sir Ken Robinson offers one view on what schools should be for. He argues that, in the way that the education system is currently organised, many schools kill children's creativity. His talk and the animated presentation challenge all of us to think about what schools are for and how we would wish to change them and about our purposes as teachers.

REFERENCES

Brunetti, G (2006) Resilience under Fire: Perspectives on the Work of Experienced, Inner City High School Teachers in the United States. *Teaching and Teacher Education*, 22(7): 812–25.

Cuddy, A (2012) Your Body Language Shapes Who You Are. *TEDGlobal*. [online] Available at: www.ted.com/talks/amy_cuddy_your_body_language_shapes_who_you_are?language=en (accessed 30 July 2015).

Goleman, D (1995) *Emotional Intelligence: Why It Can Matter More Than IQ*. London: Bloomsbury.

Guinott, H (1972) *Between Teacher and Child: A Book for Parents and Children*. New York: MacMillan.

Hargreaves, A and Fullan, M (2012) *Professional Capital: Transforming Teaching in Every School*. New York: Routledge.

Hobson, A J and Malderez, A (2013) Judgementoring and Other Threats to Realizing the Potential of School-based Mentoring in Teacher Education. *International Journal of Mentoring and Coaching in Education*, 2(2): 89–108.

Mansfield, C, Beltman, S, Price, A and McConney, A (2012) Don't Sweat the Small Stuff: Understanding Teacher Resilience at the Chalkface. *Teaching and Teacher Education*, 28(3): 357–67.

Oswald, M, Johnson, B and Howard, S (2003) Quantifying and Evaluating Resilience-Promoting Factors: Teachers' Beliefs and Perceived Roles. *Research In Education*, 70(1): 50–64.

Paavola, S, Lipponen, L and Hakkarainen, K (2004) Models of Innovative Knowledge Communities and Three Metaphors of Learning. *Review of Educational Research*, 75: 557–76.

Patchen, T and Crawford, T (2011) From Gardeners to Tour Guides: The Epistemological Structure Revealed in Teacher-generated Metaphors of Teaching. *The Journal of Teacher Education*, 62(3): 286–98.

Probst, H, Boylan, M, Nelson, P and Martin, R (2014) Early Career Resilience: Interdisciplinary Insights to Support Professional Education of Radiation Therapists. *Journal of Medical Imaging and Radiation Sciences*, 45(4), 390–8.

Sachs, J (2003) *The Activist Teaching Profession*. Maidenhead: Open University Press.

Sammons, P, Day, C, Kington, A, Gu, Q, Stobart, G and Smees, R (2007). Exploring Variations in Teachers' Work, Lives and Their Effects on Pupils: Key Findings and Implications from a Longitudinal Mixed-method Study. *British Educational Research Journal*, 33(5): 681–701.

Seligman, M (2011) *Learned Optimism*. New York: Random House.

Sfard, A (1998) On Two Metaphors for Learning and the Dangers of Choosing Just One. *Educational Researcher*, 27(2): 4–13.

Sfard, A (2008) *Thinking as Communicating: The Growth of Discourses, and Mathematizing (Learning in Doing: Social, Cognitive and Computational Perspectives)*. Cambridge: Cambridge University Press.

White, J and Gardner, J (2012) *The Classroom X-Factor: The Power of Body Language and Nonverbal Communication in Teaching*. Abingdon: Routledge.

10 Successfully applying for a secondary ITE place

Bhavna Prajapat and Steve Roberts

INTRODUCTION

This chapter guides you through the process of making an application to a chosen training pathway. The previous chapters of this book and the reflective tasks will have helped prepare you to make an application. The application process can seem daunting and complicated, but we will show how you can increase your chances of being successful. This chapter includes helpful advice from student teachers and it gives advice on each of the following stages of the process:

o   gaining your first school experience;

o   identifying your training needs;

o   knowing where and when to apply;

o   writing the all-important 'personal statement'; and

o   preparing for the interview.

WHY IS SCHOOL EXPERIENCE NECESSARY?

When you think about your own years in school as a pupil, your experience of schooling was shaped, more or less, by the context of that time. As knowledge, skills and economic conditions are changing, education is also changing and you need to be aware of current practices. Many applicants have experience in TEFL or TESOL, either in the UK or abroad and, while this may be useful, it is no substitute for going into a mainstream school in the UK. Other experiences of working with secondary age pupils in out-of-school contexts (eg youth work, running arts workshops or coaching sports teams) can show commitment to working with young people. Whatever your experience may be, it is important to arrange time in school to observe the atmosphere, culture and systems that are part of the day-to-day management of large groups of pupils and their learning. Notice particularly the contribution of the additional support staff that makes a school function – a school is not just made up of teachers.

Thomas and Pattison (2014) describe informal learning as things pupils learn out of school and, in this case, your school observation visit is informal learning in the school context (see Chapter 5). You can anticipate that this experience will provide new insights that will inform your application and training providers will want to discuss this experience with you at interview.

Ideally, you need to organise your school experience before you submit your application. Looking back at Chapter 4 will help you think about the types of school that you are less familiar with. Find out as much as possible about the school before making contact. Look at the school's website and find out about its ethos, uniform, timings for the week/term, curriculum, extra-curricular activities, catchment area, location, admissions policy, exam results, dress code for teachers and any other information you can find. Schools generally understand that most ITE providers will ask for some kind of recent school experience as part of the application process for becoming a teacher. Although different providers may vary slightly in their expectations, the more schools you observe the better your understanding will be. In making a request to visit any school, remember that there are times when schools are very busy, particularly towards the end of term time and during the examination period.

If you are well prepared for the observation time, then you will learn more from this experience. You should look at the requirements of the national curriculum and see how the school's curriculum relates to that policy. Explore some examination specifications for your subject specialism and find out which one the school/department has chosen for its Key Stage 4 curriculum and how it is managed. Going into a school will provide opportunities where you can:

o   observe pupils in class and out of class;

o   observe pupils entering and leaving a classroom and the school premises;

o   observe and talk to teachers;

o   observe your subject being taught and how the learning is structured in the different age phases (Key Stage 3 and Key Stage 4);

o   find opportunities to make connections with any post-16 links that the school might have;

o   look at pupils' work, notebooks or folders;

o   explore the teaching resources and learning frameworks being utilised;

o   make notes of the online resources being used (you could follow them up later);

o   observe the relationships that teachers build with their classes;

o   see the strategies the teacher uses to support pupils who are struggling;

o   experience the general day-to-day running of the school;

o   attend the school assembly and observe how it is managed;

o   observe how issues that arise are dealt with;

o   think about the hierarchical structure of the school and how it helps in the running of the school; and

o   decide if you are suited to working in a secondary school.

Observing a teacher in the classroom is not as straightforward as it might sound. Never forget that being allowed to observe a professional educator working with children is a privilege. You should remember that what you will see is the tip of the iceberg and underpinning that teacher's classroom practice is *'evaluation, routine, preparation, planning, personality, professional judgement, subject knowledge and professional knowledge'* (Green and Leask, 2013, p 15). It is easier to understand what teachers do in the classroom when you have the chance to discuss it with them and ask questions, though you should be aware that this is not always possible.

Reflective task

School experience will be discussed at interview. Make notes on the following questions.

o What will you be able to talk about?

o What did you learn about schools?

o What did you learn about teaching?

o What did you learn about yourself?

o What surprised you about the way pupils learn in the classroom?

YOUR APPLICATION FOR ITE

Which training provider should you choose?

Chapter 3 outlines the different pathways into teaching and explains the differences between undergraduate, postgraduate (PGCE/PGDE), School Direct Tuition (SDT) and School Direct Salaried (SDS) pathways.

Having made the choice of the pathway you wish to follow into teaching, you then need to look for providers that suit your needs. You can search for providers and courses on the UCAS website (www.ucas.com/ucas/teacher-training/find-training-programme). You will need to decide, depending on your individual circumstances, whether you are willing to travel or change location to secure a place on a course. The more flexible you are on this matter, the greater your choice. You can also look at the Complete University Guide (CUG) online (www.thecompleteuniversityguide.co.uk/league-tables/rankings) where you will find information on Schools of Education that are involved in validating different pathways into ITE. You will have to look at university and school websites to compare pathway and course details.

Universities and schools, working in partnership, will host open days (or open evenings) where you can meet and talk with tutors about the training opportunities they provide. For subjects with a strong practical element you will want to know what facilities are available.

The Department for Education organises *Train to Teach Roadshows* at various locations and you can find a calendar of events on their website (www.gov.uk/government/organisations/department-for-education). Regional *Train to Teach* events are helpful if you want to find out about what pathways local providers can offer, especially if you are able to offer more than one subject specialism and are uncertain which you would like to pursue.

Where and when do you apply?

Applications for ITE are currently handled by UCAS and all the relevant information about the application process can be found on their website: www.ucas.com/ucas/teacher-training/apply-and-track.

The process opens in the autumn and has two stages: *Apply 1* and *Apply 2*. You will only be concerned with Apply 2 if you are not made an offer or you do not accept an offer of a training place in Apply 1. You can choose up to three pathways/courses/providers at the same time. It is a competitive process, and admissions tutors are looking for strong candidates who have the potential to be good and outstanding subject specialist teachers in a very short space of time. They know that taking someone into training who is not yet ready to succeed would be a mistake.

It is a good idea to make your application as soon as you can. Increasing your knowledge of schools and gaining extra experience can continue after you have made your application.

Applicants for postgraduate pathways are not required to have as much professional experience as applicants to pathways that only provide the QTS qualification, but experience of working in schools and professional expertise from other careers is still valued. SDS applicants do not have to demonstrate achievement at postgraduate level and may not have to write academic assignments, but providers know that the qualities of critical reflection and intellectual insight are not 'optional extras' for a teacher.

> *Becoming a skilled teacher demands inter alia commitment, energy, diligence, tenacity and intelligence. Not everyone has these qualities.*
>
> (Chambers et al, 2010, p 122)

What are the essential details of the application?

The UCAS application form for all pathways will ask you to include:

o   the qualifications required for the particular ITE pathway;

o   your personal statement in support of your application;

o   two references supporting your application;

o   your declarations regarding disability and fitness to teach;

o   your declaration regarding any criminal convictions.

The questions that admissions tutors ask themselves when reading any application are likely to include the following:

o   Does this candidate have the basic qualifications that are the minimum requirements for entry to the teaching profession? (ie English and mathematics at grade C and higher or equivalent).

o   Do this candidate's qualifications meet the advertised minimum expectations for this pathway/course? (ie a degree for postgraduate courses, although not necessarily in their chosen specialism and A levels or equivalent for undergraduate courses).

○ Does the candidate have sufficient subject knowledge for their chosen specialism?

○ Does the candidate's personal statement give a good indication of his/her potential as a teacher?

○ Does the candidate's personal statement show his/her potential to become an enthusiastic advocate for the specialist subject?

○ Do the references support and enhance the application with some credibility and authority?

All applications are given careful consideration. Admissions tutors will want to interview anyone who meets most of their expectations. If your application does not provide clear answers to these questions, you may be rejected without interview.

The UCAS website gives plenty of advice and guidance on how to fill in your application and it doesn't have to be completed all in one sitting.

The Skills Tests

In addition, in England, you will have to pass the Skills Tests in Literacy and Numeracy. It is not necessary to have passed these tests before you apply, or before you are interviewed, but you will not be able to start your training until you have passed both tests.

The Skills Tests can be a surprising challenge, even for well-qualified graduates. Make sure you have prepared for these tests by using the practice materials that are available online and in books (for example, Lawson et al, 2015).

Do not be put off if your practice attempts produce discouraging results; you may have to work at completing tasks within the time limits, particularly if you have not thought about such matters for a while. You are only allowed to re-sit the tests twice. After a third failed attempt, in either the literacy or numeracy test, you will not be able to take the tests again, or start your training, for another two years.

You can find out about the tests online at: sta.education.gov.uk/

○ Literacy Test practice material:

sta.education.gov.uk/professional-skills-tests/literacy-skills-tests

○ Numeracy Test practice material:

sta.education.gov.uk/professional-skills-tests/numeracy-skills-tests

What do you write in a 'personal statement'?

The personal statement is your first opportunity to introduce yourself to the admissions tutor, so you should make sure it creates a positive impression. At secondary level, admissions tutors are looking for particular commitment to the specialist subject, in addition to your general interest in teaching and education, and working with young people. You need to articulate your reasons for wanting to teach your specialist subject. You might focus, for example, on how your own experience of being taught the particular subject has shaped your life and career to date, or been of benefit to you personally.

Explain how your personal, professional or academic experience informs your understanding of the subject and your ideas on how it might be taught effectively. Other experiences, such as having management responsibilities in another field, are also relevant. If you have had particular training or qualifications, you should explain how they would support you in teaching the subject. When writing about your recent school experience, or working with young people in other contexts, identify the reasons why it has been beneficial to you and reflect on the skills, knowledge or understanding you have gained from the experience. A list of your accomplishments or achievements is not particularly interesting for its own sake; you must reflect on how those accomplishments might be turned into advantages in your chosen career.

Reflective task

Before you start writing your personal statement, make a list of the important attributes and qualities you have that make you a good candidate for the teaching profession. Can you answer each of the questions below in no more than one sentence?

○   Why do you want to be a teacher?

○   Why do you want to teach your subject?

○   Why will you be a good subject specialist?

○   What are you hoping to get out of your ITE?

The sentences you write to answer these questions might form the basic structure of your personal statement.

Student teacher voice

Rebekah: *It is very difficult to write about yourself in a concise and personal way. Getting it read by others can be slightly disheartening if bits have to be altered or even taken out. Once you have made several drafts, you might feel it has lost the personal touch. However, I don't think that's the case. Those who read it will pick out the points that are important and the tutors will then see everything they need to!*

Adele: *The UCAS form seems geared towards recent graduates. If you've come from a previous career it's hard to fit into the boxes on the generic form. Use the personal statement to just 'tell*

> *it how it is'; include your strengths, even if they don't fit into what you 'should' write about. I did this; some places said 'No' straight away, but I believe the right one said 'Yes', as that was the university tutor who could accommodate my journey from my previous career to my new career in teaching.*
>
> **Robert:** *Some universities have fantastic career services. The university where I did my undergraduate degree was brilliant at helping me write my personal statement and giving me professional advice on the entire application process, including getting prior school experience.*

Admissions tutors will be paying close attention not only to what you have written about but also to the technical accuracy of your expression. All teachers have to be good communicators and you should aim to write in a style that observes the conventions of Standard English, without being unnecessarily formal. The best personal statements give a lively sense of the author's personal 'voice' and make interesting reading. The weaker personal statements tend to be uninspiring and, in the worst cases, incoherent. Clarity of expression is often neglected by applicants who do not check their personal statement carefully before submitting the application. Even if you are not applying to be a teacher of English, a personal statement with too many basic errors in punctuation, spelling and grammar will not make a good impression or succeed.

You have limited space to complete your personal statement (UCAS allow 4000 characters and spaces, or 47 lines of text). You will need to check that the UCAS 'word count' has been used appropriately, especially if you 'copy and paste' from another document or file.

While there are different ways of writing a personal statement that reveal your personal attributes in a positive light, there are things that you should try to avoid, as they rarely make you look good.

○ If you claim to be passionate about your subject without demonstrating a strong commitment to your subject in the rest of your statement, your claim will look like a hollow boast.

○ If you repeat the same words, phrases or sentence structures in a short piece of writing, it creates the impression that you have a limited vocabulary.

○ Aim for a direct style; avoid unnecessarily complicated or lengthy sentences; and be positive about your achievements (without exaggeration).

Research focus

Savage, J and Fautley, M (2010) *Secondary Education Reflective Reader*. Exeter: Learning Matters.

Your personal statement needs to be informed by an awareness of general issues in education. This book gives you an idea of some of the most important questions to think about. Teaching and learning in every subject is underpinned by teachers' understanding of how pupils learn. You will have some understanding of the ways you learn yourself and will have opinions about what is involved in learning. As part of your training, you will be expected to investigate how philosophy and education research present a range of different theories and perspectives on learning. Familiarising yourself with some of the main schools of thought will enhance your application as well as informing your discussion at interview.

Who should be your referees?

Anyone who can comment with some credibility and authority on your potential to be a successful teacher can be asked to provide a reference in support of your application. People with whom you have a personal relationship (family members, friends or partners) should not be asked to act as your referee. Applicants for SDS pathways will need at least one reference from an employer. If you have graduated from university in the last five years, you should include one academic reference. It is sometimes difficult to secure an academic reference a long time after graduation. The strongest references always come from someone who can comment on your character and suitability for the profession in some detail, based on relatively recent experience of working with you in a professional capacity. It is your responsibility to approach and secure the agreement of your referees before you make the application.

Reflective task

Think about people with whom you have a professional or academic relationship.

○   Who understands your professional capability and potential as a teacher?

○   What will they be able to say about you that will enhance your application?

○   Have you discussed with them the possibility of you becoming a teacher?

What else does your provider need to know?

The application will give you an opportunity to declare any particular needs you may have in relation to a disability. You are not obliged to do so, but you should not worry that a declaration will count against you. Providers have to ensure that their admissions procedures are fair, non-discriminatory and comply with all the relevant equality legislation. Informing the provider enables them to ensure that reasonable adjustments are made, where necessary, for interview tasks and helps them understand your training needs. A more thorough and detailed health check will take place after you have accepted an offer.

You will be asked to disclose details of any criminal convictions. Having a criminal record is not automatically going to stop you being a teacher, but you can anticipate that matters of this nature will be discussed in confidence with you, if necessary. You should always check with providers before you apply, if you have particular concerns.

How long does it take to get a reply?

When your application is in the system, you can track the progress of your application via the UCAS website (www.ucas.com/ucas/undergraduate/apply-and-track/track-your-application). Admissions tutors receive a lot of applications and will make their decisions promptly.

If your application is successful, you will receive a letter or email inviting you to attend an interview. You should respond to the invitation and indicate whether you will be attending or not. If you later find you cannot or do not wish to attend the interview, it is an important courtesy to inform the institution, as they will be able to offer that interview appointment to another candidate. You may find yourself being called for interview at the same time in different places. If there is a conflict of dates, you may be able to rearrange the interviews to enable you to attend both.

Your letter of invitation will normally give you clear and detailed instructions on how to prepare. Interview procedures vary and each subject specialism will have its own way of doing certain things. For example, Art and Design candidates can expect to be asked to produce a portfolio of original work and this might be complicated to present. You might have a website, or your portfolio may exist in some other form. If you are unsure, contact the institution and ask for advice on portfolio content and presentation.

Every moment of the time spent in the institution at interview will inform the decisions about your future. It is important to be punctual and know where you are supposed to report. On arrival, you will be asked to confirm your identity with either a driver's licence or a passport, and to provide the original certificates that confirm your qualifications. Turning up without these documents will make you look disorganised and may result in the interview being postponed. If certificates are lost, it is your responsibility to organise replacements or other authorised confirmation from the examination-awarding bodies.

The purpose of the interview for the admissions tutor is to confirm the potential shown in your application that makes you a good candidate for the course. You should also have a clear purpose in your own mind; you need to know whether this course and the people who will be involved in your training are the right choice for you. Have a list of questions with you on the day to inform your decision.

INTERVIEWS

What happens at your interview?

The interview process will provide opportunities for you to demonstrate the qualities that support success in ITE:

○ commitment to working with young people;

○ understanding of the teaching profession, its challenges and rewards;

○ ability to reflect on and learn from experience;

○ depth and breadth of subject knowledge;

○ ability to communicate, in spoken and written language;

○ personal resilience.

Make sure that you have followed the advice and guidance given on preparing everything the institution asks of you. You should anticipate the need to dress appropriately for a professional employment interview. While there is no formal dress code for the teaching profession, in most schools, professional and 'business-like' appearance is an established norm.

It is quite common for a number of candidates to be interviewed on the same day. You may be part of a large crowd of applicants for different pathways and you will probably receive a lot of information about the institution and the course in both informal discussion and formal presentations.

School Direct interviews usually take place in school, but you may also have to attend an interview at the university. Some providers hold joint or group interviews, which can be a little intimidating, as this kind of forum can challenge your communication skills. You will be asked to complete a brief written task during the interview day. It is not uncommon for candidates to be given some kind of discussion task as an opportunity for observers to assess ability in social contexts. This can be nerve-wracking, as you may feel you are being asked to interact in a co-operative manner with people you think you are competing against, but this situation is far less stressful than teaching a classroom of teenagers. It provides an opportunity to show how well you can lead and respond in discussion, how well you can contribute to developing ideas or intervene decisively at certain moments, or how well you cope with others who are more dominant, assertive, compliant or reticent in discussion.

Reflective task

○ How well do you cope with interview situations? Think about previous interviews and how you responded to the pressure of 'interrogation'? Do you become nervous? Do you gabble or babble? Does your mind go blank?

○ What coping strategies do you need to develop? Is there someone who might help you practise articulating your responses?

Student teacher voice

Rebekah: *I think in general the application process, especially the interview, is very daunting, but it gives you an insight into the year to come. It is a very challenging course, but extremely worth it in the end!*

James: *The interview was perhaps the hardest part, due to a lack of previous interviews. I tried to prepare for the possible questions that could come up and made sure that my personal statement was not exaggerated.*

Tom: *Prepare for questions and be aware of current changes in education. Answer truthfully and honestly. Don't try to lie about gaps in your subject knowledge!*

What might you be expected to do at your interview?

You may be asked to make a brief presentation on a given topic, or you may be asked to teach a lesson on a particular theme. In these cases, if you are in school, you can anticipate that you will be asked to work with pupils in some way, though not all schools will expect you to teach a full lesson to pupils. You could be asked to reflect on this at a later stage of the interview.

If asked to present, make sure you follow advice given on style and content. Stick to time limits (and make sure you have rehearsed the presentation, allowing for the nervous impulse that will speed your speech up under the duress of the moment). Address the people present in the room, your audience, and interact with them in a relaxed manner. A presentation is an opportunity for you to be seen in the communication mode that secondary school teachers use in almost every lesson:

o   addressing a group of people as an audience, engaging and holding attention, articulating a train of thought;

o   communicating ideas clearly and succinctly;

o   signposting the talk for the audience with verbal emphasis and appropriate gestures; summarising and managing visual aids or resources.

Try not to over-rely on a prepared script or prompt cards, as this will tend to make your talk rather dull. Have the confidence to know your major points and talk freely around your subject; it will always be more interesting and engaging.

You will be given the opportunity to respond to questions in a personal interview which will probably be with one or two tutors or school-based colleagues. Some interview panels can have more people present. You will have an opportunity to talk about your reasons for coming into teaching; what has made you choose your subject as your specialism in secondary school; and what you have learned about teaching and learning from your recent experiences in school. You should always answer with your own thoughts, making use of your preparation and research without trying to give a 'correct' or complete answer. The interviewer will ask supplementary questions, probing to see how much thought you have given to your future in teaching.

What do you know about your subject and how it is taught?

Chapter 6 discusses the importance of subject knowledge in secondary teaching. The interview will provide an opportunity for you to discuss your subject knowledge and how it might need to develop. You can prepare by familiarising yourself with current policy and practice in teaching your subject; looking at the way the subject is defined (or not) by the national curriculum; and keeping up to date with policy debates in your subject through news media and online journals. Your interviewer is not expecting you to know everything about your subject or the appropriate methods for teaching it, but you should be aware of your areas of expertise and the limitations of your personal knowledge. You should also show you are aware that educational beliefs are open to challenge and debate:

> The construct of the 'good teacher' has teacher knowledge as a fundamental component; but teacher knowledge is contested. Policy makers offer one version, articulated through such documents as Teachers' Standards. However, it might be argued that this version of teacher knowledge, largely defined by national curriculum and assessment demands, does not constitute the whole of what teacher knowledge might encompass.
>
> (Brindley, 2013, p 393)

You should bear in mind that your personal knowledge of the subject is only part of what constitutes 'subject knowledge' in teaching; each subject will have its own discourse about how knowledge, skills and understanding are acquired by pupils in that subject and there is often debate about what might be the best ways for teachers to make pupils more successful in their learning. You should think about the most challenging aspects of your subject for pupils at different ages and stages of development. Interviewers tend not to be impressed by candidates who have not thought about what is involved in teaching pupils who do not yet share their personal passion or enthusiasm for the subject. You should articulate your view of the benefits of studying your subject beyond the immediate requirements of the assessment system. There are few simple answers to the complex questions that teachers face on a daily basis:

> Should teachers in secondary schools focus primarily on helping pupils acquire subject knowledge so they pass examinations with good grades, enabling them to find a job or go to university? Or do teachers also have a responsibility to contribute to pupils' overall well-being and prepare them for life in a wider sense?
>
> (Sanderse et al, 2015, p 195)

How prepared are you for the realities of teaching?

You can anticipate that the interviewers will want to know how good you are at coping with stressful situations. They will want reassurance that you have the resilience and tenacity to cope with the demands of the teaching profession. If you lack experience in the classroom, it might be appropriate to speak about other professional or academic experiences that were difficult or stressful for you, and how you overcame those difficulties. Here the interviewer will be looking for you to reflect on how you coped with the situation; whether you sought assistance or guidance from others; and what you learned about managing in challenging circumstances. It is worth thinking about how much teachers rely on their colleagues for support in schools, in all sorts of formal and informal ways.

At the end of the interview you will be given an opportunity to ask questions. Do not leave the interview without checking your list of questions. The main question you should ask yourself at this point is 'would I accept the offer of a place here?' If you are uncertain, then you may need to ask some other questions to try and work out what is causing your hesitation. If you are certain you would accept, then all you have to do is wait for the admissions tutor's decision to be communicated back to you via the UCAS system. You will receive formal notification in writing of the offer, and any conditions attached. When all your chosen providers have informed you of their decisions, you will have ten days to make your decision to confirm your acceptance of one offer.

What happens after the interview?

If you are unsuccessful at interview, you may or may not receive an indication of the reasons for the decision to reject your application. You can request some feedback from the admissions tutor on your performance in the interview and you may receive some helpful suggestions about how to improve your chances of success in subsequent interviews. Take notice of the advice given. If you are advised to gain further experience before reapplying, you should perhaps reconsider whether you are ready, at this moment, for a career in teaching.

Assuming that your interview is successful and you accept the offer, your training provider will direct you to pre-course materials and recommendations will be given on how to prepare for the course. Keep an eye open for email communications from your training provider, as tutors may wish to establish a dialogue with you before the course starts. After that, with your offer confirmed and all conditions satisfied, you can plan to make good use of your last moments of relaxation before you join the teaching profession.

CONCLUSION

Your first professional year will be intense – physically, mentally and emotionally – so make sure you are fully rested and prepared for the challenges ahead. If you are happy that you are in the right place, working with the right people, and you are enthusiastic about the opportunities your course provides, you are more likely to learn how to teach well and become an excellent teacher.

Progress checklist

Check you have completed the following steps to prepare your application for ITE:

1. Contact a school to arrange observation and experience.

2. Reflect on experience to identify key questions.

3. Identify personal training needs (eg subject knowledge enhancement, knowledge of theories of learning, knowledge of behaviour management, disabilities and special needs and other educational priorities).

4. Identify the pathways and providers to which you will apply.

5. Check particular pathway specifications and ensure your qualifications match expectations and minimum requirements.

6. Check that you have original certificates for all relevant qualifications.

7. Write the personal statement.

8. Proofread the personal statement.

9. Contact your referees, discuss your intention to apply for ITE and secure their agreement to provide a reference in support of your application.

10. Go online and complete the UCAS application.

11. Review literacy and numeracy Skills Tests support materials and guidance.

▶▶ **TAKING IT FURTHER**

Burn, K, Hagger, H and Mutton, T (2015) *Beginning Teachers' Learning: Making Experience Count.* Northwich: Critical Publishing.

This book closely follows the professional journey of 25 teachers through their first few years in secondary education.

Coe, R, Aloisi, C, Higgins, S and Elliot Major, L (2014) *What Makes Great Teaching? Review of the Underpinning Research.* Centre for Evaluating and Monitoring (CEM), Durham University and The Sutton Trust. [online] Available at: www.suttontrust.com/researcharchive/great-teaching/ (accessed 31 July 2015).

This report is a review of over 200 pieces of research identifying evidence-informed practices that support learning (as well as those that are harmful and have no grounding in research).

Green, A and Leask, M (2013) What do Teachers Do? in Capel, S, Leask, M and Turner, T (eds) *Learning to Teach in the Secondary School: A Companion to School Experience.* 6th ed. London: Routledge.

This chapter provides you with an insight into the daily routines and range of work teachers engage in.

Lawson, J, Charles, A and Kreft, T (2015) *Success: Passing the Professional Skills Tests for Teachers.* Northwich: Critical Publishing.

This text provides support for anyone thinking of taking, or about to take, the Professional Skills Tests in numeracy and literacy.

Blogs and twitter feeds

Department for Education Get into Teaching: @getintoteaching

UCAS Online: @ucas_online

REFERENCES

Brindley, S (2013) Teacher Education Futures: Compliance, Critique, or Compromise? A UK Perspective. *Teacher Development: An International Journal of Teachers' Professional Development*, 17(3): 393–408.

Chambers, G, Hobson, A and Tracey, L (2010) 'Teaching Could be a Fantastic Job But ...': Three Stories of Student Teacher Withdrawal from Initial Teacher Preparation Programmes in England. *Teachers and Teaching: Theory and Practice*, 16(1): 111–29.

Green, A and Leask, M (2013) What do Teachers Do? in Capel, S, Leask, M and Turner, T (eds) *Learning to Teach in the Secondary School: A Companion to School Experience.* 6th ed. London: Routledge.

Lawson, J, Charles, A and Kreft, T (2015) *Success: Passing the Professional Skills Tests for Teachers.* Northwich: Critical Publishing.

Sanderse, W, Walker, D and Jones, C (2015) Developing the Whole Child in an Age of Academic Measurement: Can This Be Done According to U.K. Teachers? *Teaching and Teacher Education*, 47: 195–203.

Savage, J and Fautley, M (2010) *Secondary Education Reflective Reader.* Exeter: Learning Matters.

Thomas, A and Pattison, H (2014) Informal Learning, in Pollard, A *Readings for Reflective Teaching in Schools.* 2nd ed. London: Bloomsbury.

11 Conclusion

Andy Davies and Mel Norman

The main aim of this book has been to support you in making the decision of whether to become a secondary teacher. We have sought to address this through a balanced account of different aspects of both learning to teach and also being a secondary school teacher. This final chapter summarises the key themes that are discussed in the book. It then considers secondary teaching in a contemporary context, reflecting on current employment prospects, opportunities for CPD and the potential impact of ongoing reforms to secondary education.

KEY THEMES

While written from the individual perspectives of different authors, the chapters of this book have highlighted certain key themes for those who commit to getting into secondary teaching:

1. The importance of developing self-awareness in preparation for your teaching career.

2. The need to hold and apply your specialist subject knowledge.

3. The necessity to understand the all-embracing nature of the commitment needed to become a successful practitioner.

Having read Chapter 2 you will have engaged with the question of whether secondary teaching is for you, and Chapter 3 will have led you through the various routes it is possible to follow to gain your teaching qualification. Chapter 4 outlined the significant influence of government policy on the education system in England that you need to appreciate before embarking on learning to teach. Chapter 5 discussed the nature of professional learning, complemented by Chapter 6 which focused on the importance of specialist subject knowledge for secondary teaching. Chapters 7, 8 and 9 underlined the broad nature of secondary teaching, dealing with issues surrounding behaviour management, being a form tutor, involvement with the PSHE curriculum, safeguarding pupils and maintaining your own well-being in a highly intensive yet very rewarding career as a teacher. Hopefully, having made the decision that secondary teaching is the right career for you, Chapter 10 guided you through the process of applying for a place on a secondary ITE programme.

We hope that the information provided, issues discussed and illustrative material presented in the form of teachers', student teachers' and others' voices in the book have stimulated your thoughts about secondary teaching. We also hope you now have the tools to make an informed decision about whether to become a secondary teacher and, if appropriate, to successfully apply for one of the current ITE pathways to QTS.

EMPLOYMENT PROSPECTS

The employment prospects for secondary teachers in England are currently very good. The numbers of children in primary schools started rising in 2010 and are projected to increase until at least 2024 (DfE, 2015). Naturally this will lead to a follow-on rise in the numbers of children moving through the secondary sector coupled with an increase in numbers at post-16 now that all young people have to continue in some form of education until the age of 18. Government policy regarding the EBacc and the new 'Progress 8' (see Chapter 4) means there is an increased need for teachers with the specified subject specialisms to enable schools to meet these curriculum demands. The impact of the Pupil Premium (see Chapter 4) has meant that schools have the facility to spend some of the additional funding on employing additional teaching staff.

In spite of excellent employment prospects there will still be competition for jobs so you need to present your individuality, just as you will do when applying for an ITE programme. You need to give examples of the impact you will have on the pupils you teach and to demonstrate how you feel you will develop as a teacher. It is essential that you reflect on your resilience and your commitment to the holistic dimension of the job of teaching and show how you are prepared to be part of the school community, not just a teacher of a subject.

As regards applying for jobs there are a number of different ways in which you may find out about job opportunities. Local authorities still provide online information about vacancies in their schools, and there are an increasing number of agencies which advertise jobs for schools. Publications such as the *Times Educational Supplement*, *Guardian Education* and *The Independent* advertise posts on a weekly basis. If you are hoping to live and work in a particular area, there is nothing to stop you writing to every school within a certain radius from where you will be living to alert them to the fact that you are seeking a teaching post, and enclosing a current CV.

CONTINUING PROFESSIONAL DEVELOPMENT

During your NQT year and beyond, there will be opportunities for you to engage with continuing professional development (CPD). These opportunities, such as programmes run by professional subject associations, may keep you up to date with your subject specialism. The *Council for Subject Associations* (CfSA) is an organisation that acts on behalf of the different subject associations. By accessing the member section of the CfSA website you can find links to the different subject associations – and we would strongly encourage you to do so. Subject associations provide access to valuable resources for use in your teaching and the opportunity to collaborate in networks with other teachers of your subject specialism. Contact details are included in the references below.

Once you are established as a fully qualified teacher you may decide to study towards a Masters degree. Teachers who engage in such study find it a powerful way to expand their knowledge of education, develop their practice and benefit from opportunities for further professional development. You may be interested in supporting others who want to enter the profession, so developing your mentoring skills by undertaking shadowing within your school or following a short course on mentoring might be an appropriate goal for you. Research shows that mentors as well as mentees can benefit greatly from being part of mentoring relationships (Hobson et al, 2009). A variety of organisations offer a range of CPD opportunities which you should review as and when you feel ready for further engagement with study. You may get some funding and/or time from your school for CPD but this varies from school to school. However, it is important to note that the Teachers' Standards (DfE, 2013) identify the expectation that professional development will be ongoing throughout your career, and that following meaningful professional development opportunities can be good for your well-being as well as helping you to become and remain a good, excellent or outstanding teacher.

FUTURE CHANGES

School-led teacher education has been in the ascendance in England since at least 2010. The current government's policy is to create the conditions for schools to be more autonomous in how they recruit and train teachers. This may mean that recruitment into teaching is not distributed evenly across different regions or that there may be too many teachers trained in one area and too few in another part of the country. However, it is hard to predict what will happen given that many schools are applying to work as School Direct providers but may only apply for small numbers of training places. There is a current concern, voiced strongly by the CfSA (House of Commons Education Committee, 2013), that school-based secondary training programmes may lead to shortages in recruitment and that the expertise and rigour provided by university-based subject specialists is sometimes lacking. To this end, many school alliances are linked into partnerships with universities that provide the validation for the Masters-level postgraduate qualification, still generally considered the most valuable teaching qualification both in Britain and abroad, should you be thinking of spending some time teaching overseas.

Increasing numbers of schools are part of academy chains, teaching school alliances or federations of schools working together (as mentioned in Chapters 3 and 4). This creates conditions for groups of schools to recruit teachers to a 'pool' for an alliance or academy chain. It may be that schools will increasingly group together to recruit across a particular region.

It is important to remember that academy and free schools are entitled to appoint people to teaching posts who do not have a teaching qualification (see Chapter 4). With the Conservative government's promise of the establishment of another 500 free schools (Morgan, 2015) and the extension of the academy network, it might be asked whether there is any point in undertaking a teaching qualification. We strongly believe that gaining a teaching qualification is still the best route into a successful teaching career both in England and abroad, and we hope that the chapters in this book have encouraged you to follow a programme that will lead to a recognised qualification in teaching and properly prepare you for the complex and challenging nature of the work of a secondary teacher. Would you want to engage the services of a solicitor or see a doctor or a dentist who had not gained appropriate education, training and qualifications?

CONCLUSION

The authors of this book have sought to provide you with a comprehensive account of secondary teaching, to enable you to make a series of informed decisions relating to a possible career as a secondary teacher. We would not wish to mislead you and suggest that training to become and actually being a secondary teacher are easy: they can be extremely challenging and possess a number of potential downsides. Nonetheless, in our experience as teachers and teacher educators, we are also aware that the distinctive nature of secondary teaching with its key ingredients of subject specialism, working with young adults and the potential for exciting collaborations with other education professionals can lead to a hugely rewarding career, and it is a genuine honour and privilege to be part of the teaching profession.

Teaching is vital for society, and being a teacher is an enormous responsibility that has a real impact on you and the world around you – now and in the future. The importance of committed, well-qualified and critically reflective practitioners cannot be overestimated. Individual teachers make a positive difference to the lives of the pupils they work with on a daily basis. We hope to have inspired some of you to take the step of embarking on a teacher training programme and following a career in secondary teaching. Good luck!

REFERENCES

Council for Subject Associations (CfSA) (n.d.) Council for Subject Associations homepage. [online] Available at www.subjectassociation.org.uk (accessed 2 August 2015).

Department for Education (DfE) (2013) *Teachers Standards: Guidance for School Leaders, School Staff and Governing Bodies (Introduction updated June 2013)*. London: Department for Education.

Department for Education (DfE) (2015) *National Pupil Projections – Future Trends in Pupil Numbers: July 2015*. London: Department for Education.

Hobson, A J, Ashby, P, Malderez, A and Tomlinson, P D (2009) Mentoring Beginning Teachers: What We Know and What We Don't. *Teaching and Teacher Education*, 25(1): 207–16.

House of Commons Education Committee (2013) Written Evidence Submitted by the Council for Subject Associations. *Commons Select Committee Written Evidence, Parliament*. [online] Available at: www.publications.parliament.uk/pa/cm201314/cmselect/cmeduc/371/371we18.htm (accessed 1 July 2015).

Morgan, N (2015) *Free Schools Drive Social Justice*. Press release. [online] Available at: www.gov.uk/government/news/free-schools-drive-social-justice-nicky-morgan (accessed 29 June 2015).

Appendix

Department for Education

Teachers' Standards

PREAMBLE

Teachers make the education of their pupils their first concern, and are accountable for achieving the highest possible standards in work and conduct. Teachers act with honesty and integrity; have strong subject knowledge, keep their knowledge and skills as teachers up-to-date and are self-critical; forge positive professional relationships; and work with parents in the best interests of their pupils.

PART ONE: TEACHING

A teacher must:

1 Set high expectations which inspire, motivate and challenge pupils

- establish a safe and stimulating environment for pupils, rooted in mutual respect
- set goals that stretch and challenge pupils of all backgrounds, abilities and dispositions
- demonstrate consistently the positive attitudes, values and behaviour which are expected of pupils.

2 Promote good progress and outcomes by pupils

- be accountable for pupils' attainment, progress and outcomes
- be aware of pupils' capabilities and their prior knowledge, and plan teaching to build on these
- guide pupils to reflect on the progress they have made and their emerging needs
- demonstrate knowledge and understanding of how pupils learn and how this impacts on teaching
- encourage pupils to take a responsible and conscientious attitude to their own work and study.

3 Demonstrate good subject and curriculum knowledge

- have a secure knowledge of the relevant subject(s) and curriculum areas, foster and maintain pupils' interest in the subject, and address misunderstandings
- demonstrate a critical understanding of developments in the subject and curriculum areas, and promote the value of scholarship
- demonstrate an understanding of and take responsibility for promoting high standards of literacy, articulacy and the correct use of standard English, whatever the teacher's specialist subject
- if teaching early reading, demonstrate a clear understanding of systematic synthetic phonics
- if teaching early mathematics, demonstrate a clear understanding of appropriate teaching strategies.

4 Plan and teach well structured lessons

- impart knowledge and develop understanding through effective use of lesson time
- promote a love of learning and children's intellectual curiosity
- set homework and plan other out-of-class activities to consolidate and extend the knowledge and understanding pupils have acquired
- reflect systematically on the effectiveness of lessons and approaches to teaching
- contribute to the design and provision of an engaging curriculum within the relevant subject area(s).

5 Adapt teaching to respond to the strengths and needs of all pupils

- know when and how to differentiate appropriately, using approaches which enable pupils to be taught effectively
- have a secure understanding of how a range of factors can inhibit pupils' ability to learn, and how best to overcome these
- demonstrate an awareness of the physical, social and intellectual development of children, and know how to adapt teaching to support pupils' education at different stages of development
- have a clear understanding of the needs of all pupils, including those with special educational needs; those of high ability; those with English as an additional language; those with disabilities; and be able to use and evaluate distinctive teaching approaches to engage and support them.

6 Make accurate and productive use of assessment

- know and understand how to assess the relevant subject and curriculum areas, including statutory assessment requirements
- make use of formative and summative assessment to secure pupils' progress
- use relevant data to monitor progress, set targets, and plan subsequent lessons
- give pupils regular feedback, both orally and through accurate marking, and encourage pupils to respond to the feedback.

7 Manage behaviour effectively to ensure a good and safe learning environment

- have clear rules and routines for behaviour in classrooms, and take responsibility for promoting good and courteous behaviour both in classrooms and around the school, in accordance with the school's behaviour policy
- have high expectations of behaviour, and establish a framework for discipline with a range of strategies, using praise, sanctions and rewards consistently and fairly
- manage classes effectively, using approaches which are appropriate to pupils' needs in order to involve and motivate them
- maintain good relationships with pupils, exercise appropriate authority, and act decisively when necessary.

8 Fulfil wider professional responsibilities

- make a positive contribution to the wider life and ethos of the school
- develop effective professional relationships with colleagues, knowing how and when to draw on advice and specialist support
- deploy support staff effectively
- take responsibility for improving teaching through appropriate professional development, responding to advice and feedback from colleagues
- communicate effectively with parents with regard to pupils' achievements and well-being.

PART TWO: PERSONAL AND PROFESSIONAL CONDUCT

A teacher is expected to demonstrate consistently high standards of personal and professional conduct. The following statements define the behaviour and attitudes which set the required standard for conduct throughout a teacher's career.

- Teachers uphold public trust in the profession and maintain high standards of ethics and behaviour, within and outside school, by:
  - treating pupils with dignity, building relationships rooted in mutual respect, and at all times observing proper boundaries appropriate to a teacher's professional position
  - having regard for the need to safeguard pupils' well-being, in accordance with statutory provisions
  - showing tolerance of and respect for the rights of others
  - not undermining fundamental British values, including democracy, the rule of law, individual liberty and mutual respect, and tolerance of those with different faiths and beliefs
  - ensuring that personal beliefs are not expressed in ways which exploit pupils' vulnerability or might lead them to break the law.

- Teachers must have proper and professional regard for the ethos, policies and practices of the school in which they teach, and maintain high standards in their own attendance and punctuality.

- Teachers must have an understanding of, and always act within, the statutory frameworks which set out their professional duties and responsibilities.

Index